"'Leaders are to be holy.' As a disciple of Maxie Dunnam's latest book, *Christian Leadership*, this affirmation is not only bold but thoroughly Wesleyan. To root a teaching on leadership in the spiritual principle of sanctification is to root us in our richest soil. With a mix of practical wisdom, stories, and lived-out teaching, Maxie calls us to a spiritually disciplined life, an alive-in-Christ faith, and a heart that is both obedient and surrendered. By making this clarion call, Maxie challenges us to what he himself has lived for decades. Thank you, Maxie, for your witness and for the gift of your wisdom as you reflect on a lifetime of servant leadership."
—Carolyn Moore, pastor, Mosaic Church, Evans, GA

"Maxie Dunnam reflects from a lifetime of perhaps unprecedented experience in church leadership. The book's range of insights, especially about vocation and the leader's spiritual formation, will root and inform many careers. Essential reading for a generation...or longer."
—George G. Hunter, distinguished professor emeritus, Asbury Theological Seminary, Wilmore, KY

"Maxie Dunnam has been a role model and mentor in my life for more than four decades. He remains relevant and prophetic in defining Christ-centered servant leadership in a post-Christian culture. *Christian Leadership* is a 'must read' for younger and older ministry leaders alike."
—Mike Slaughter, pastor emeritus, Ginghamsburg Church, Tipp City, OH; chief strategist, Passionate Churches, LLC

"*Christian Leadership* is in a league of its own. This is not just one more leadership book. It has depth, history, personal experience, solid biblical and theological foundations, and an invitation to 'prophetic intention wed to pastoral attention.' It should be required reading in all seminaries as well as for those currently serving in vocational ministry."
—Jo Anne Lyon, ambassador, general superintendent emerita, The Wesleyan Church

"Filtered through more than sixty years of parish, institutional, and academic ministry, Maxie Dunnam paints a portrait of Christian leadership that is grounded in scripture, rooted in primal Methodism, and translated for our twenty-first-century challenges and opportunities."
—Jorge Acevedo, lead pastor, Grace Church, a multi-site United Methodist congregation, Southwest FL

"Each generation produces a handful of leaders whose voices ring above the rest. Maxie Dunnam provides such a voice. A book on Christian leadership by Maxie is not simply a must read; it is a gift to the church."
—Shane L. Bishop, distinguished evangelist, The United Methodist Church; senior pastor, Christ Church, Fairview Heights, IL

"In *Christian Leadership*, Maxie Dunnam takes us on a stroll, introducing us to the classic Christian leaders of the past. Along the way, we become friends with these heroes and realize that Maxie is so comfortable with these giants of the faith because he is one himself."
—Jim Cowart, founding pastor, Harvest Church, Warner Robins, GA

"*Christian Leadership* is an important contribution to the challenges and opportunities of leadership in both church and parachurch contexts. Anchored to a solid understanding of current organizational theory, Maxie—out of his years of experience as a pastor, denominational executive, and seminary president—brings his unique applications to bear on the realities of guiding religious work in these times of seismic change in our culture's core values and commitments."
—David J. Gyertson, associate provost and dean, Beeson School of Practical Theology, Asbury Theological Seminary, Wilmore, KY

"Maxie Dunnam provides a wise, pastoral word about leadership that is born of experience and a passion for people. Dunnam challenges us to open our minds, hearts, and lives to being sharpened and used by God—just as he created us. Maxie's personal transparency, passion for making a difference, and deep kingdom commitment inspire all of us to be leaders who are ambassadors of grace, hope, and truth."
—Steven G. W. Moore, executive director, M. J. Murdock Charitable Trust, Vancouver, WA

MAXIE DUNNAM

CHRISTIAN LEADERSHIP

speaking to God for the people
speaking to the people for God

Abingdon Press
Nashville

CHRISTIAN LEADERSHIP

Copyright © 2019 by Abingdon Press

All rights reserved.

No part of this work may be reproduced or transmitted in any form or by any means, electronic or mechanical, including photocopying and recording, or by any information storage or retrieval system, except as may be expressly permitted by the 1976 Copyright Act or in writing from the publisher. Requests for permission should be addressed in writing to Permissions, Abingdon Press, 2222 Rosa L. Parks Blvd., Nashville, TN 37228-1306, or permissions@abingdonpress.com.

This book is printed on acid-free paper.

Library of Congress Cataloging-in-Publication Data has been requested.

978-1-5018-8311-8

Scripture quotations unless noted otherwise are taken from the Common English Bible, copyright 2011. Used by permission. All rights reserved.

Scripture quotations noted JBP are taken from The New Testament in Modern English by J. B. Phillips copyright © 1960, 1972 J. B. Phillips. Administered by The Archbishops' Council of the Church of England. Used by Permission.

Scripture quotations noted KJV are from The Authorized (King James) Version. Rights in the Authorized Version in the United Kingdom are vested in the Crown. Reproduced by permission of the Crown's patentee, Cambridge University Press.

Scripture quotations noted NEB are taken from the New English Bible, copyright © Cambridge University Press and Oxford University Press 1961, 1970. All rights reserved.

Scripture quotations marked (NIV) are taken from the Holy Bible, New International Version®, NIV®. Copyright © 1973, 1978, 1984, 2011 by Biblica, Inc.™ Used by permission of Zondervan. All rights reserved worldwide. www.zondervan.com The "NIV" and "New International Version" are trademarks registered in the United States Patent and Trademark Office by Biblica, Inc.™

Scripture quotations noted RSV are from the Revised Standard Version of the Bible, copyright © 1946, 1952, and 1971 National Council of the Churches of Christ in the United States of America. Used by permission. All rights reserved worldwide. http://nrsvbibles.org/

19 20 21 22 23 24 25 26 27 28—10 9 8 7 6 5 4 3 2 1
MANUFACTURED IN THE UNITED STATES OF AMERICA

Contents

Introduction	vii
1. The Vocation of Leadership	1
2. The Shape of Our Vocation	15
3. Lessons from the Saints	31
4. What Is Good Ministry?	47
5. The Persons We Are and the Institutions We Serve	61
6. The Preacher and Preaching	71
7. Out and About	87
8. Taking Care of Ourselves in the Everyday	103
9. Little Foxes That Spoil the Vines	113
10. Time: It Is Ours to Receive, Use, and Manage	129
11. Staying Alive All Our Ministry Life: Will You Finish Well?	139

Introduction

I am eighty-four years old at this writing and still active in ministry, serving as Minister at Large at Christ United Methodist Church, Memphis, Tennessee. I answered the call to preach when I was seventeen. I've been preaching all my life. I still feel I'm doing what I was created to do.

My call into Christian leadership began as vague stirring in my mind in the summer between my junior and senior year of high school, when I participated in a three-day youth retreat. One of the worship services was on the banks of Lake Lynn, a small lake near where we lived. The preacher, David McKeithen, the pastor of the Methodist Church, got into a small jon boat, rowed out about forty feet, stood in the boat, and preached. I was alarmed because I could not imagine him being able to stand in the boat and preach without it capsizing. The kind of preaching I had been exposed to would not allow a preacher to stand still anywhere; they were always moving about, shouting, dramatically waving their arms, slapping the Bible, or pounding the pulpit. But that was not the case with this man's preaching. It was not loud shouting, punctuated by body movement, but thoughtful and well-stated explanation and reflection on Scripture. There was passion, but it was not expressed so much with emotion as with his obvious conviction about what he was saying. There was no question about it; he was calling us to discipleship, to faithfully follow Jesus. It was invitational; low-key, but challenging.

He suggested that Christ may be calling some of us into full-time Christian service, possibly to be a pastor or to serve in the mission field. He made it clear, though, that every one of us was called to be Christian full-time, while some may have a full-time vocation within the church. This was a new thought. Unable to sleep that night, I pondered what that would look like for me; but more, whether the Lord was calling me. From that night on, the thought never seemed far from my mind.

As I became more involved in the youth group, I had more opportunity to observe the pastor because he spent a good bit of time with the group. The Spirit was working as I began to wonder what his life was really like. A thought kept recurring: I think I'd like to be like him.

Those thoughts were sketchy, and I shared them with no one. I was intent on finishing high school and going to college. My four-month summer job after high school gave me plenty of time to think and dream. The call to preach became a bit more clamoring. Though I did not share this with anyone, by the time I got to college, the calling pervaded my thoughts. I also had time with the pastor and his family. I asked a lot of questions, read some books he recommended. I never felt any pressure, or had any thought that he might be leading me into the ministry. I asked him a lot of questions about doctrine and church governance. He paid attention, gave me time, invited me into his home, and I became a small part of his family.

I went to college in the fall following high school graduation. I dropped out after two quarters, not finishing an entire academic year. The call was stirring within. I got a job, but worked only two months, my mind in turmoil as I wrestled with what was becoming more clamorous, what I perceived to be God's call. I had saved enough money to pay my tuition, so I returned to college, determined to do whatever I needed to make clearer my call and how to pursue it.

I experienced a life-giving truth: verbalizing something gives it a reality that is not there until the word is spoken. In all my wrestling with the call, I had not shared it with anyone, yet deep within, by now I had made the decision to give myself to a life of preaching. After the notion had tumbled around in my mind in muddled confusion for months, with weeks when I could think of nothing else, I simply said to David, who had become my pastor, "I think I'm being called to preach."

David had a wry, telling smile; it was one of the most beautiful things about him. But his smile that day was more telling than it could have ever been before. "I know," he said, "I've just been waiting for you to acknowledge it."

Those words gave solid substance to my struggle; and when David asked, "Are you going to answer?" and I said yes, my calling became real.

When I said yes to God, through David, the trajectory of my life was set.

Introduction

For me, the ultimate expression of my calling in terms of my vocation was preaching. I had my first appointment when I was nineteen, a three-point student charge in rural Mississippi. I was still a college student at the University of Southern Mississippi. After college, I shared in organizing a church in Atlanta and served as pastor for two years while a seminary student.

Sixty-two years since graduation from seminary at Candler School of Theology, I have served in full-time ministry. Apart from ten years with The Upper Room as Director of Prayer and Spiritual Formation, and World Editor, and ten years as president of Asbury Theological Seminary, I have been the pastor of congregations in rural areas, small towns, suburban, and city settings. I have had the awesome privilege and responsibility of "planting"—being the organizing pastor—of three congregations. These have been glorious years—rich and rewarding; demanding and at times trying.

I have often been asked to preach and teach about ministry, the nature of calling, leadership, and preaching. I have done this in all sorts of ways: seminary teaching, lecturing, conference speaking, magazine articles, and random chapters in books.

As I was writing my memoir, *God Outwitted Me*, it became clear that I should reflect and write more specifically about leadership and the practice of ministry.

I write particularly for young men and women who are feeling a call to life and leadership within the church, but also for those serving as leaders who may feel a need to hear from one who has been on the journey for many years, and is as excited about ministry as at any time in his life. It is also my hope and prayer that my reflections will enable laypersons and congregations to perceive more expansively and deeply the meaning of ministry; and perhaps be called to a deeper commitment to corporate ministry in the life of their congregations, as well as individually in their communities.

On the surface, there is something presumptuous about a person such as I—a person not unlike you—audaciously daring to speak of, and even for, God. There are times when I am smitten by the whole notion of ministry—the irony, the humor, the incongruity of it all—me, here, speaking for God.

As I began working on these reflections about Christian leadership, Jerry, my wife, told me a story about comedian Groucho Marx. He was given the opportunity to be part of the famous Friars' Club, which was considered to be quite an honor. Marx's reply was, "I don't care to belong to any club that will have me as a member" (*The Groucho Letters* [New York: Simon and Schuster, 2007], 8).

That's the way I sometimes feel about ministry. How is it that I'm here? What did God have in mind—how could it be that the Lord would put his hand on my shoulder and beckon me in this specific call? It helps me to remember that Paul voiced this same kind of concern:

> We don't preach about ourselves. Instead, we preach about Jesus Christ as Lord, and we describe ourselves as your slaves for Jesus' sake. God said that light should shine out of the darkness. He is the same one who shone in our hearts to give us the light of the knowledge of God's glory in the face of Jesus Christ.

> But we have this treasure in clay pots so that the awesome power belongs to God and doesn't come from us. We are experiencing all kinds of trouble, but we aren't crushed. We are confused, but we aren't depressed. We are harassed, but we aren't abandoned. We are knocked down, but we aren't knocked out. We always carry Jesus' death around in our bodies so that Jesus' life can also be seen in our bodies. (2 Cor 4:5-10 CEB)

One way I've stayed alive in ministry, and maintained a sense of balance or perspective, is by constantly appropriating this witness of Paul: the image of the treasure in a clay pot. I seek to stay focused on the treasure, staying aware that I am an earthen vessel in which it is carried.

My prayer is that my reflections will not only inspire and encourage but provide some guidance for persons navigating this awesome journey of leadership.

Chapter 1

The Vocation of Leadership

Some say that leaders are born, not made. That is partially true. Some people are born with natural gifts that make for good leadership. Yet, some leaders are born in the midst of adversity. Others emerge because a situation demands it. Think of parenting. What parent has been trained to be a parent before the first child arrives? We discover leadership abilities we never even thought about as we are "forced" to guide and protect our children from the cradle until they leave us "empty nesters."

Because leadership is so crucial in all of life, great attention has been given to this essential dynamic, especially in the past twenty-five years. Little time passes before another "must read" leadership book comes from the press. The church has been served well by pastors and ministry leaders paying attention to the need for good leadership, with some of them contributing to the spate of "leadership books" coming to us.

However, in too many cases not enough attention is paid to spirituality and/or spiritual formation when writers and conference leaders offer help to pastors and ministry leaders. Pastors and others who guide and direct different ministry expressions are leaders—but they are *Christian* leaders.

The role that this type of leader assumes differs from almost any other leadership role in the world. We are called to witness to the truth of the gospel, and to provide soul care for those who sin and struggle. We have the responsibility of providing guidance for the church, which is always at a point of not yet being where the Holy Spirit is calling her. Our vocation calls us to discern God's truth, always keenly aware that our discernment of truth may not be God's truth. Humility must pervade our search and expression of truth, because God alone remains God. Thus our understanding is to a marked degree always fragile and fallible.

The uniqueness of Christian leaders does not invalidate general leadership principles aimed at the CEO of a business, or the president of a university, or a general officer in the military. It does mean that we think of Christian leadership vocationally, from a Christian perspective. Though oftentimes viewing a leader's role as a stereotypical caricature and within a limited generality, secular leaders count the leader's role as a privilege and expect to be ministered unto; Christian spiritual leaders are privileged not to be served but to serve, concerned primarily not with their own welfare but the welfare of others. A person can have a brilliant mind and possess expansive leadership gifts and skills, but without commitment and Christian spirituality he or she will not be the leader Christ is calling for and the Christian movement needs.

Two Pictures

Let's compare two literary portraits of the Christian leader. The first is out of the rich treasury of Celtic spirituality. It's a portion of Patrick's own account of his pilgrimage.

> I, Patrick, am the most unlearned and the lowest of all the faithful. My father was a deacon, and my grandfather a priest. At the age of sixteen I was taken captive and shipped to Ireland, along with thousands of others.
>
> When I arrived in Ireland, I was sent to tend sheep. I used to pray many times each day; and as I prayed, I felt God's love fill my heart and strengthen my faith. I had to stay all night in a hut on the mountain, looking after the sheep, and each day I would wake to pray before dawn in all weathers—snow, frost, and rain. I remained as a slave in Ireland for six years.
>
> One night when I was asleep, I heard a voice speaking to me. It told me that a ship was waiting to take me home. I awoke, and immediately ran down the mountain, and hurried to the coast. I found a ship about to set sail; and although the captain did not want to take me, one of the old sailors smuggled me aboard.
>
> I was overjoyed to see my family again, and at first thought I should never leave them again. But one night I had another dream in which a voice spoke to me. The voice implored me to return to Ireland, and preach the gospel. When I awoke I felt as if I were a slave again—but now God was my master. (Robert Van De Weyer, *Celtic Parables* [Nashville: Abingdon, 1999])

This picture immediately grounds us, and reveals our understanding of the vocation of leadership from a Christian perspective. There is calling and anointing.

A second literary portrait comes from *The Spoon River Anthology* by Edgar Lee Masters. This anthology is a collection of eulogies of people who are buried in two cemeteries in the same town. One cemetery is for the common people and the other for the special ones. Father Malloy was buried in the cemetery for special people, and this is what is said about him:

> You are over there, Father Malloy,
> Where holy ground is, and a cross marks every grave,
> Not here with us on the hill—
> Us of wavering faith and clouded vision
> And drifting hope, and unforgiving sins.
> You were so human, Father Malloy,
> Taking a friendly glass sometimes with us,
> Siding with us who would rescue Spoon River
> From the coldness and the dreariness of village morality.
> You were like a traveler who brings a little box of sand
> From the waste about the pyramids
> And makes them real and Egypt real.
> You were a part of and related to a great past,
> And yet you were so close to many of us.
> You believed in the joy of life.
> You did not seem to be ashamed of the flesh.
> You faced life as it is,
> And as it changes.
> Some of us almost came to you, Father Malloy,
> Seeing how your church had divined the heart,
> And provided for it,
> Through Peter the Flame,
> Peter the Rock. ([New York: Macmillan, 1921], 203)

It's obvious that Father Malloy was a leader, a Christian leader, among the people in Spoon River. It's a wonderful picture of the mingling of flesh and spirit, sin and grace, human weakness baptized with something sacred, dreariness and despair diminished by hope. It's a testimony to the need for leadership, and the genuine appreciation people have for one who can inspire and provide vision: "You were like a traveler who brings a little box of sand from the waste about the pyramids and makes them real and Egypt real."

Calling and Career

With those two pictures in mind, we reflect on the vocation of leadership. Vocation comes from the Latin, *vocātiō*. Two simple definitions are "a strong desire to spend your life doing a certain kind of work (such as religious work)" and "the work that a person does or should be doing."

The Latin term *vocātiō* has in it the word *vox*, meaning "voice," and the related word *vocāre*, meaning "to call." So when we think of vocation, it is easy to think of calling, invitation, summons; and of gaining one's voice.

Vocation is calling. It is knowing the truth, obeying God, and being guided by God in the particular expression of our life's work.

Paul and his interpreters in letters to the early churches make a big deal about this. In Ephesians 4 he contends that each of us is graced according to the measure of Christ's gifts. This is in the context of the unity of the church: "You are one body and one spirit, just as God also called you in one hope.

There is one Lord, one faith, one baptism, and one God and Father of all, who is over all, through all, and in all" (Eph 4:4-6 CEB). Then there is that marvelous description of vocation in the church: "He gave some apostles, some prophets, some evangelists, and some pastors and teachers. His purpose was to equip God's people for the work of serving and building up the body of Christ" (Eph 4:11-12 CEB).

Paul begins this illuminating and challenging discussion with this plea: "Therefore, as a prisoner for the Lord, I encourage you to live as people worthy of the call you received from God" (Eph 4:1 CEB). The KJV translates this, "Walk worthy of the vocation wherewith ye are called." So God does not say, "Be good" or "Be spiritual." God says, "Walk with me."

> Walk in the way of love. (Eph 5:2 NIV)
>
> Walk as children of light. (Eph 5:8 KJV)
>
> Walk worthy of the Lord. (Col 1:10 KJV)
>
> Let us walk honestly. (Rom 13:13 KJV)
>
> We walk by faith, not by sight. (2 Cor 5:7 KJV)

These teachings about living a trustworthy and faithful life worthy of our Lord in the Letters to the Ephesians, Colossians, Romans, and Corinthians reflect the Lord's word to Abraham when Abraham was ninety-nine years old and was making covenant with him: "I am El Shaddai. Walk with me and be trustworthy" (Gen 17:1 CEB). "So "walk worthy of our calling."

Sometimes I sense too much confusion between calling and career. Though the words are sometimes used interchangeably, they are actually very different in meaning and should not be confused.

"Career" is the term we use most often to describe what enables one to make a living, meaning usually a job or some form of employment, whether in industry, a profession, or some other field. One's career hopefully carries with it remuneration and benefits that support one's livelihood and desired lifestyle.

Bishop Edward Lewis Tullis (1917–2005) tells of going to a church one Sunday morning to preach. He arrived early and decided that he would go to the Sunday school simply to see what was happening. When he entered the assembly room and took a seat on the back row, a little girl, about nine years old, stood up to give a recitation about characters in the Old Testament. When she came to Enoch, she said something the bishop never forgot: "Enoch was such a close friend of God that one day they took a walk together and Enoch never came back."

We don't know much about Enoch from the Bible. We know that he was the son of Cain, who had killed Enoch's uncle, Abel. When Enoch grew up, he married and had children. When he was sixty-five years old, he became the father of Methuselah, the oldest man ever to live. Then "Enoch walked with God and disappeared because God took him" (Gen 5:24 CEB).

Jesus, who taught his followers by walking with them, used the image of walking with the Lord many times. He issued the call to take a walk with the imperative, "Follow me." When

Jesus defined the meaning of discipleship, he said, "All who want to come after me must say no to themselves, take up their cross, and follow me" (Matt 16:24 CEB).

These expressions of "walk," as a challenging metaphor for our calling and our faithful way of living, offer promise and direction for those who would be spiritual leaders, distinguishing between career and calling.

The Secret

Off and on, for over forty years, my daily ritual in devotional prayer time has included a thought said to myself. Sometimes I speak it aloud, sometimes I simply register it in my consciousness. The sentence prayer is, "Maxie, the secret is simply this, Christ in you, yes Christ in you, bringing with him the hope of all the glorious things to come."

That's from the Phillips paraphrase of the Letter to the Colossians. Paul is describing his calling and his identity by saying,

> I myself have been made a minister of this same Gospel, and though it is true at this moment that I am suffering on behalf of you who have heard the gospel, yet I am far from sorry about it. Indeed, I am glad, because it gives me a chance to complete in my own sufferings something of the untold pains for which Christ suffers on behalf of his body, the Church. For I am a minister of the Church by divine commission, a commission granted to me for your benefit and for a special purpose: that I might fully declare God's word—that sacred mystery which up to now has been hidden in every age and every generation, but which is now

as clear as daylight to those who love God. They are those to whom God has planned to give a vision of the full wonder and splendour of his secret plan for the sons of men. And the secret is simply this: Christ in you! Yes, Christ in you bringing with him the hope of all glorious things to come. (Col 1:24-27 JBP)

The Christians in Colossae were apparently challenged by early Gnosticism. The Gnostics gained their name from the Greek word *gnosis*, meaning knowledge. By claiming a superior and esoteric wisdom, they asserted that God was separated from the world, distantly so, and had not directly created the world. Matter was evil and spirit was good. Since God was spirit and therefore good, the evil material world could have no contact with God.

This Gnostic teaching challenges the most basic Christian understanding of Jesus as the incarnation of God. The Christian teaching that God came in the human flesh of Jesus Christ, loved, forgave, and reconciled the world, could not be believed, argued the Gnostics. If Jesus was God's son, he could not dwell in the flesh because all matter is evil. So, they taught, Jesus must have been an "emanation" from God—at most, one of a gradation of angels. Following that line of reasoning, they contended that Jesus did not really live as a man; his suffering on the cross was not real; there was no point in the Resurrection, because he had never really lived as a material being in evil human flesh.

So the letter to Colossae, which circulated among other churches too, seems to be an early objection to this particular deception that denigrated the adequacy of the all-sufficient

Christ. In Colossians 2:8, the letter says, "See to it that nobody enslaves you with philosophy and foolish deception, which conform to human traditions and the way the world thinks and acts rather than Christ" (CEB).

The Gnostics have no special knowledge, Paul says. There is a secret, a mystery, but it is an open one, open to those of faith. In all his dealing with humanity, God has been working on a plan for the redemption of humankind. In response to the Gnostic notion of the secrets of the universe being revealed in their special knowledge, Paul said, "No, that isn't it. The secret is not in a philosophy, but in a person—the person of Jesus Christ." And the mystery of the secret is that Christ can dwell in you and me.

Paul's great definition of a Christian was "a person in Christ." He used that phrase "in Christ" or its equivalent at least 172 times in the Pauline Letters. His most vivid description of his own life in Christ was written to the Galatians: "I have been crucified with Christ and I no longer live, but Christ lives in me. And the life that I now live in my body, I live by faith, indeed, by the faithfulness of God's Son, who loved me and gave himself for me" (Gal 2:20 CEB). In one of the boldest prayers every prayed, Paul interceded, "I ask that Christ will live in your hearts through faith. As a result of having strong roots in love, I ask that you'll have the power to grasp love's width and length, height and depth, together with all believers. I ask that you'll know the love of Christ that is beyond knowledge so that you will be filled entirely with the fullness of God" (Eph 3:17-19 CEB). What a revelation: that you and I may attain the fullness of God, "which is Christ living in you, the hope of glory" (Col 1:27 CEB).

It was from this revelation, this gospel, that Paul says, "I was made a minister" (Eph 3:7 KJV). This distilled essence of Paul's teaching means that God's mysterious secret, which "has been hidden for ages and generations" (Col 1:26 CEB), which men and women have sought to probe and decipher for thousands of years, has now been revealed. That secret is Christ, but more, it is "Christ in you, the hope of glory." This is more than a career; this is a calling. Spiritual leaders share in the mystery of Christ and they are called to share the secret.

The clue to the whole Christian experience, the core of the gospel, is that this Christ, by whom and through whom all things were created; this Christ, who is before all things and in all things; this Christ, in whom God was pleased for all his fullness to dwell; this Christ, the firstborn over all creation, the image of the invisible God; this Christ who has primacy over all things, in whom all things hold together; this Christ, who is the head of the church and who will stand at the end of time and be the final judge and triumphal Lord. This Christ offers to live in us through the Holy Spirit.

All Christians share in the secret, but some are called to the special opportunity of sharing the mystery. This privilege is almost as overwhelming as our share in the mystery itself. We are called—given responsibility—allowed the awesome opportunity of sharing the mystery with others. If Paul was speaking, rather than writing, we imagine him shouting excitedly: "For I am a minister of the Church by divine commission, a commission granted to me for your benefit and for a special purpose: that I might fully declare God's word—that sacred mystery which up to now has been hidden in every age and every generation, but which is now as clear as daylight to those who love God" (Col 1:25-27 JBP). Not only are we the recipients, we are the communicators of the mystery.

Sharing the mystery of grace is the task of every Christian, but it's especially the calling of ordained clergy. Ordination means far more than we can plumb, but in its basic form it means that we are called, called by Christ and set apart by the church.

The Work of God

The disciples once asked Jesus, "What must we do in order to accomplish what God requires?" Jesus replied, "This is what God requires, that you believe in him whom God sent" (John 6:28-29 CEB). Our calling, the work that defines everything else about our vocation as leaders is to believe in the one God has sent. Our relationship to God is the deepest thing about us. That being right, other things will be right; that being wrong, nothing else can be as right as it might be.

Our bedrock grounding as leaders is in God. This grounding comes through deliberate and explicit attention to God through prayer and self-reflection. Leadership as vocation, Christian leadership, begins with self-leadership, clarifying our own heart, soul, and mind in order to find and show that our most basic identity, and our deepest and most concrete security lie in God—not in success, or in pleasing someone else, not in being seen as a good person, or being loved by a congregation or the faith community we lead, but in God.

Many leaders, especially those in the Wesleyan tradition, recall the bold assertion of John Wesley: "Give me one hundred preachers who fear nothing but sin and desire nothing but God, and I care not a straw whether they be clergymen or laymen, such alone will shake the gates of hell and set up the kingdom of heaven on earth" (letter to Alexander Mather in Bristol, Aug. 6, 1771, *The Letters of the Rev. John Wesley,* MA. vol. 6 [London: Epworth Press], p. 272).

Wesley recognized that God chooses to use preachers, lay or clergy, to effect God's kingdom work in the world. The persons God uses, the ones who make the difference, are those completely yielded to God. All the capacities they possess are open to use for God's purposes. They are, by their relationship to God, exercising a divine call to leadership as a way of love and a way of living.

I often punctuate my life with this prayer, "O Lord, give me the grace to be completely yours." Psalm 42:1-2 (CEB) expresses this same yearning:

> Just like a deer that craves streams of water,
>   my whole being craves you, God.
> My whole being thirsts for God, for the living God.

Passion and yearning are essential dynamics for keeping our calling and sense of vocation alive. I practice a regular self-checkup on my yearning and passion, asking,

- How does my present level of passion for the Lord compare to those early years when I first sought and knew him; those months when I struggled with God's call upon my life?
- Do the people I serve recognize in me a pervasive desire to see God more clearly, love him more dearly, and follow him more nearly?

The Puritan writers and preachers talked about developing our passion for the Lord as "heart work." John Flavil, a seventeenth-century English Puritan, said, "The greatest difficulty in conversion is to win the heart to God; and the greatest difficulty after conversion is to keep the heart with God." Heart work is hard work, yet where we focus our passion determines the direction of our lives.

In the next chapter we will discuss the shape of our leadership calling. From the biblical perspective, we will examine that shape in terms of our calling as prophet/priest.

Chapter 2

The Shape of Our Vocation

A few years ago I was smitten by a text from Ezekiel 2:4-5 that I heard in the ordination service of the Free Methodist Church. "I'm sending you to their hardheaded and hard-hearted descendants, and you will say to them: The Lord God proclaims. Whether they listen or whether they refuse, since they are a household of rebels, they will know that a prophet has been among them" (Ezek 2:4-5 CEB).

Ezekiel is sharing his personal story of God coming to him in a vision, and calling him into service. The account is vivid but complex. It is easy to get lost in the imagery. Ezekiel sees the Lord's glory coming down from heaven. It is so overwhelming that he falls on his face. But the Lord will not let him remain there: "Human one, stand on your feet, and I'll speak to you" (Ezek 2:1 CEB).[1] And the Lord does speak.

---

1. The Lord calls and addresses Ezekiel as a human being to speak for God. The words *human*, *human being*, or *human one* are a frequent Old Testament translation of the Hebrew *bene' 'adam*, that is, a person who descended from the first human, Adam. In the New Testament, Jesus is the new Adam, because followers of the Christ are new humans, born again. The Greek *huios tou anthropou* (rendered in the KJV Gospels as "Son of Man") is actually an awkward or wooden way to translate the Hebrew idiom *bene' 'adam*.

The message, which Ezekiel is to preach, is given to him in a kind of scroll. Thus Ezekiel receives his appointment. It is not a promising situation. Not the planting of a new church that is sure to grow in an exciting fashion. Not to be the senior pastor of First Church, downtown, which has tremendous influence in the entire community. Not an appointment to a rapidly growing church in suburbia. Not to lead a national faith-based ministry that is growing in influence and is about to go international. It is a hard call, and God makes it clear. In exercising his prophetic office, Ezekiel will have to preach to deaf ears and dwell among scorpions. There is no prospect of success laid on the prophet in the initial call to ministry. And that burden of probable failure for his community continues to increase as God continues to speak.

Even so, the call carries with it the power of support. The Lord makes the prophet's face harder than flint. The message of doom that Ezekiel is to proclaim is given to him to eat. That message is written in a scroll, which exists already in heaven, and it tastes as sweet as honey. From now on, the prophet is entirely on God's side, and the person and the message are the same. Which brings us back to the heart of the text: "Whether they listen or whether they refuse…they will know that a prophet has been among them."

After all these years, ever since that ordination service, I haven't been able to get away from that text. It has been, and continues to be, troublesome truth, burning in my mind and heart—calling me to regular personal assessment of my own witness and ministry, judging my failure, and challenging me to a deeper commitment. To what degree do people know, when I have been among them, that a prophetic presence was there?

Old Testament scholar Gerhard von Rad says that more than any other prophet, Ezekiel is influenced by the priestly religious life of Israel, and indeed his prophetic ministry is a priestly one. He observes that Ezekiel is the first prophet consciously to enter this particular sphere of activity, which may be described as the "cure of souls" (*The Message of the Prophets* [New York: Harper & Row, 1972], 200). His calling was not just the traditional prophetic task of addressing the community and the nation—speaking the Lord's word to them—but also caring for individuals, assisting persons to recognize their own situation in God's eyes.

Ezekiel's calling to ministry suggests the shape of vocational leadership as prophet/priest/pastor, which when faithfully performed will show people that God's representative has been among them. I add the word *pastor* to von Rad's description of Ezekiel, because it names the comprehensive task of leadership by a person in a congregation. The word *pastor* refers to the kind of work that enhances the priestly and prophetic functions. In a congregation, the role of the pastor (lay or clergy) combines the prophetic and priestly functions.

> **The primary function of a prophet/priest is twofold:**
>
> speaking to the people for God and speaking to God for the people.

Chapter 2

Speaking *to* People *for* God

First, the prophet/priest speaks to the people for God. The very thought of speaking to people for God may and should make us quiver inside. But we need to keep perspective. These prophets/priests are not geniuses; if they were, we moderns could better accept the notion. Rather than geniuses they are ordinary human beings, persons like you and me, who have been called to find their voice, and in some ways anointed. They pay attention to self-leadership because they have been released from the love of self and enslaved by the love of God. They trust no longer in their own capacity but in God's power. They know that the way to life is the way of death—death to their own will and life to the will and purposes of God.

I recently asked a group of laypersons to describe the primary characteristic of their pastor, who was obviously a very effective pastor/leader. To a person, in one way or another, each responded, "He is present; we know he is with us and that he cares." He has empathy. Our prophetic/priestly function of speaking to the people for God requires identification with our people, a passion for their salvation and recovery from brokenness, and a compassion that calls for a willingness to suffer, even to die for their sake. As leaders, our people must know we care for them.

Jesus was very clear about this as he instructed his disciples. In addition to learning how to pray, the only time Jesus told his disciples that he was offering an example they were to follow was when he washed their feet. They were to be servants with intimate compassion. While washing the grime from their feet, he connected serving with suffering; he was on his way to the cross. More often than not, service does not come without suffering.

As the Lord made Ezekiel responsible, so God makes us Christian leaders responsible for the souls committed to our care in the ministries to which we are called. It was rather dramatic with Ezekiel. If he allowed the wicked to die unwarned, the Lord threatened to require their lives at the prophet's own hands. So the Lord says to him, "Human one, cry aloud, and wail" (Ezek 21:12 CEB).

As leaders, are we groaning, crying aloud and wailing, before the eyes of our people? Do they see that kind of passion and compassion flowing from our life? We can keep this passion and compassion alive by regularly asking questions like these:

- Who are the people in my congregation or community of faith who, though they are members, don't feel they really belong?
- Who are the people in my community who have yet to receive a clear message from me personally, and/or from the people I lead, that we deeply care for them and that God loves them?
- What about the poor? Am I committed to the irrefutable truth of scripture that God has taken a preferential option on their behalf? Am I speaking to people for God who, if the Lord loves one people more than any other, it is the poor?
- What of the vast segment of folks in every community—especially in our cities—for whom Christ and his church are strangers? Are we ordering

our life and worship, our ministry and mission, in a way that resonates on their turf, speaks a language they understand, and offers something that will meet their needs where they are, not where we would like for them to be?

- What about the recovering folks—those seeking freedom from addictions who self-medicate their pain? Is our church a community of welcome, a place of grace that will help them break the chains of shame and blame?

- Are there immigrants in your community? Are we and our community of faith showing hospitality to these strangers in our midst who are culturally homeless or living in fear from those who don't love others? "In welcoming these strangers, we may be entertaining angels unawares" (Heb 13:2, author's paraphrase).

"Human one, cry aloud, and wail" the Lord said to Ezekiel, and God still says to us leaders. Show the people that you care—that you speak for a God who loves us, who "forgives all your sins, heals all your sickness" (Ps 103:3)—who restores us to wholeness and gives us joy.

Speaking *to* God *for* the People

Not only do we speak to the people for God, we speak to God for the people. Our "groaning" or wailing becomes our intercession, our pleading with God on behalf of our people.

One of the symbolic actions God called for Ezekiel to perform was to lie down for a considerable time, thirteen months, first on one side and then on the other, in order to bear the guilt of the house of Israel. The Lord introduces that requirement in Ezekiel 4:4, "Now, lie on your left side, and set the guilt of the house of Israel on it. For the length of time that you lie on your side, you will bear their punishment" (CEB).

Though not a literal description of how we are to intercede, it is a powerful call to identification and suffering with and for our people, a commanding call to priestly intercession. I learned this in the deepest way when, as president of a seminary, I was led to devise a way to explicitly pray for the persons in our community. At the beginning of each year, I divided them into groups in such a way that, before the year was complete, I prayed for every person in our community.

Prior to the week that I was going to pray for particular students, faculty, and staff, I wrote them a letter inviting them to share with me their thanksgiving, as well as the particular needs for which they would like for me to pray during the week that I was giving them my prayer attention.

The experience was amazing. During a particular two-week period, I prayed for

- a young couple who had just gotten engaged
- a couple who were struggling hard to stay married
- a student's spouse, who was deaf and having difficulty getting a job
- a baby just conceived, sharing the joy of that couple
- a baby born almost blind, being fed through a stomach tube, with club feet in a cast

- a group of our students on a mission trip to Venezuela
- three professors in South Africa

I make no claims about the working out of these prayers in the lives of the people for whom I prayed, but hardly a week would pass that I didn't receive some word of affirmation and some testimony from one of them. My point, however, is that *my* life was changed, the way I did my work was altered, and the depth of my concern and compassion was intensified because I began to moan, to speak to God for these persons.

Inspired in part by this intentional prayer commitment, I came to believe that was a huge part of my leadership responsibility as president of the seminary—to be a prophet/priest presence in the community.

I also sought to make this prayer dynamic a part of the training of our students for ministry. E. M. Bounds (1835–1913) expressed my conviction:

> We believe that one of the most popular errors of the modern pulpit is the putting of more thought than prayer, of more head than of heart in its sermons. Big hearts make big preachers; good hearts make good preachers. A theological school to enlarge and cultivate the heart is the golden desideratum of the gospel. The pastor binds his people to him and rules his people by his heart. They may admire his gifts, they may be proud of his ability, they may be affected for the time by his sermons; but the stronghold of his power is his heart. His scepter is love. The throne of his power is his heart. (*Preacher and Prayer* [Kansas City, MO: Beacon Hill Press, 1946], 66)

A personal experience brings together this dual function of the prophet/priest, speaking to the people for God and speaking to God for the people. I was flying out of Tampa, Florida, late one afternoon, just before sunset. I was seated on the front row and there was an empty seat beside me. The flight attendant took a seat beside me for the take off. As we taxied out the runway, I looked and the sun was setting. The entire western sky was a blaze of glory. We took off over Tampa Bay, and I was wide-eyed in awe. It was one of the most magnificent arrays of color I had ever seen. Gold and red and pink and purple, and orange and yellow. It was a dance of color. I could hardly contain myself. "Look," I said, "look at the sunset." She glanced casually out the window but was unresponsive. She had already engaged herself with a magazine so she returned to it. Stumblingly I said, "Well, I guess you are used to that, flying all the time." She responded matter-of-factly. "Yes, it happens almost every time I fly out of here." I could tell that she was not interested in the sunset or any kind of conversation, so I returned to the book I was reading.

When we were in the air, she left her seat to do her work. Some people think that airline attendants have glamorous jobs—flying off to interesting places around the nation and exotic spots around the world. But it really is a tough job—certainly while they are on duty. Serving drinks, fending off men who have had too many drinks, tending to upset babies, being ready for every emergency—it is really a stressful and tedious job that includes walking uphill for hours.

So when this young woman left her seat, I began to pray for her. I am certainly not always that intentional, but I sensed something was going on in the life of this young woman, so I began to pray for her. It wasn't too long before we were landing in Atlanta and she took the seat beside me. I am certain of it; she was a different person. She wanted to talk, and I sensed my praying had something to do with it. Soon I was hearing the story: she would be leaving the plane in Atlanta and driving a couple of hours to visit her family in south Georgia. Just before we had taken off in Tampa, she had received the word that her mother, a cancer patient, was not going to make it much longer. This would probably be their last time together.

No wonder she had not been interested in the sunset. I was able to share my concern—the love and care of God, and to simply affirm that underneath her were his everlasting arms. She received that with thankfulness.

Now it doesn't always happen this way—but it happens just enough to cause us to know the power of it, and to give us the joy of it, and to inspire us to continue the practice. I spoke to God for a person and was given the marvelous opportunity of speaking to a person for God.

More Clarity from God's Call

I closed the first chapter with the assertion that what we set our hearts on determines the direction of our life, reminding us that heart work is hard work.

We moderns separate "heart" and "will." We associate the heart with emotion and feelings; the will with our mind, thinking, and deciding. In scripture this is not the case. The word *heart* appears 572 times in scripture. The heart represents the life-giving core of human life. It is the motivating, controlling center of our human personality, the deep inner source of passion, energy, and direction for our lives. The heart is the place of decision, the seat of the will. "As water reflects the face, so the heart reflects one person to another" (Prov 27:19 CEB). What we set our hearts on determines the direction of our lives.

This is the reason Dallas Willard insists that we meet God in our "practices." And practices are the reason our spiritual father, John Wesley, talked so much about the "means of grace." He talked about them in two ways: instituted and prudential. The instituted means of grace for staying in love with God are prayer, scripture, devotional reading, Holy Communion, fasting, and Christian conferencing (conversation). The prudential means of grace (which are general rules) are simply two: doing no harm and doing good.

Without diminishing the importance of these means of grace, or narrowing Willard's insistence on practices, I believe we act our way into Christlikeness. Of course, the means of grace (prayer, scripture, Holy Communion, Christian conferencing) and additional ones Mr. Wesley did not name (confession, generosity, solitude) are absolutely essential. Yet, I've never seen a person who prayed her way into Christlikeness. I've never seen a person who studied his way into Christlikeness. I've never seen a person who worshipped her way into Christlikeness. But I know countless people who have acted their way into

Christlikeness. Sure, they were praying people, and they studied; they were faithful in worship, practicing the means of grace, but they acted their way into Christlikeness by setting their hearts in the direction of relieving human suffering, liberating women and men in bondage, making peace with enemies, countering anger with kindness, and so forth. Our effectiveness as a leader depends on our passion for balancing piety and mercy throughout a lifetime.

Being a prophet/priest after the likeness of Jesus is not a one-time, once-and-for-all, "well, it's done" kind of thing. It's a lifelong process, and its power is cumulative.

I saw the evidence of this leadership principle in Nelson Mandela's life. As one of the presidents of the World Methodist Council, Jerry (my wife) and I had the privilege of sharing in a service when the council gave Mandela the World Methodist Peace Award for the year 2000. The service was held in Cape Town's Central Methodist Mission.

Mandela's entire life was a witness to God's guidance and support as he gave himself courageously in the fight against apartheid. It was also the witness of community and the mutual support of persons committed to the same purpose. Mandela affirmed and spoke with deep gratitude for the role The Methodist Church, especially lay preachers, played in his life.

In his presence and witness, as he responded to receiving the peace award, there was the added confirmation to what he said in his autobiography:

There was no epiphany, no singular revelation, no moment of truth; rather a steady accumulation of a thousand slights, a thousand indignities, a thousand unremembered moments, produced in me an anger, a rebelliousness, a desire to fight the system that imprisoned my people. There was no particular day on which I said, from henceforth I will devote myself to the liberation of my people; instead, I simply found myself doing so, and could not do otherwise. (*Long Walk to Freedom* [Boston: Little, Brown and Co., 1995], 109)

Mandela proved that as he walked to his car from Central Mission, where he had received the award. A small child with one leg and a crutch hobbled toward him. The security people were there to turn away that little one and others who pressed in. But Mr. Mandela motioned for the child to come to him. Almost immediately, at least twenty-five other street children pressed in around him and his car. I will never forget the light on those children's faces as they talked to this great man and felt the warmth of his welcome and smile.

What we set our hearts on, especially in the small moments on the way to somewhere else, determines the direction of our lives. We act our way into Christlikeness.

Prophetic Intention and Pastoral Attention

The prophet Ezekiel as an example also clarifies our calling and shapes our leadership function through pastoral attention and prophetic intention: we must learn to listen, stand up, and make a promise.

First, in Ezekiel 2:1, God says, "Stand on your feet, and I'll speak to you" (CEB). The lesson? We are to listen. Our reaction must always be a receptive one: "Speak, Lord. Your servant is listening" (1 Sam 3:9).

Second, after hearing the Lord tell him to stand on his feet so that God might speak to him, Ezekiel says, "As he spoke, the Spirit came into me and raised me to my feet, and I heard him speaking to me" (Ezek 2:2 NIV). Some translations (CEB, NET) translate the Hebrew (*ruakh*) as a wind that brought the prophet to his feet. Whether it is Spirit or a divine wind that propels us to our feet, it isn't our ability to do what God calls us to do, but our willingness to respond, to yield, to attempt that releases God's power.

You may experience this second lesson when God calls you to a ministry or a mission that you can't accomplish in your own strength and with your own resources. When you realize that only with divine aid will your mission be accomplished, you stay on your knees, dependent upon the Lord.

Third, a lesson about ingesting God's will.

> Then he said to me: Human one, eat this thing that you've found. Eat this scroll and go, speak to the house of Israel. So I opened my mouth, and he fed me the scroll. He said to me: Human one, feed your belly and fill your stomach with this scroll that I give you. So I ate it, and in my mouth it became as sweet as honey. (Ezek 3:1-3 CEB)

Like Ezekiel, we must become one with God's word. What we say must be matched by how we live. It is then that people will know that a prophet/priest is among them. That's what character and holiness are all about as it relates to our Christian vocation.

Tammy is responding to this call as clearly as anyone I know. She was converted and nurtured in a dynamic campus ministry at the University of Georgia. She felt God's call upon her life. But like many, she was clueless as to the shape of that call and where it might lead. She came to Asbury Theological Seminary with no money, in total dependence upon the Lord.

The summer before her last year in seminary, she went to India on a short-term mission. God confronted her there in a deeper, more profound way than ever before. She fell in love with the homeless street children in Bangalore and knew this was a part of God's calling for her life. By a series of miraculous God-incidences, she is now in India, in a compassionate ministry with little children. More than one hundred children have been loved and cared for in the "grace house" she established. Some of these children are now adults; two of them opened a café as a mission center to share the gospel, which was shared with them so compellingly by Tammy.

I have known few people who are as totally dependent upon the Lord as Tammy. She sends e-mail messages to her friends and supporters. I always read them with great joy, as well as being challenged by her commitment. Though at least thirty-five years younger than me, Tammy is a mentor. I'm learning from her simple bedrock faith and radical abandonment to Jesus. Always in her communication, there is a confession of her dependence upon the Lord, and her willingness to live sacrificially in order to fulfill God's call. In one of her e-mails (October 4, 2000) she wrote:

> I encourage you to let God take you deeper in prayer and intimacy. I know these are the "Christian catch phrases" these days. But, well…it's the truth. I guess my prayer for you is that you would go deeper with Jesus, that you would let Him wash through you like a rushing river, cleansing, soothing, filling you in every good way. Intimacy—just more of Jesus. That place where you utter a prayer and in an instant it has been answered. That place where you are convicted of yourself in sin and in the same moment encouraged and refreshed. That place in your heart where man's words can't reach, but one word from God, and you melt.

Tammy provides a clear picture of seeking God through spiritual disciplines, the thirst for holiness, and dependence upon the Lord. These things must be cultivated in the life of each leader to make us prophets/priests.

The heart of the matter is always a matter of the heart, which means a matter of the will, responding to God's call to prophetic intention and pastoral attention.

Chapter 3

Lessons from the Saints

Most of us can recall the events and crucial timing in our ministry that were watershed occasions, transition times, marking dramatic redirection or paradigm shifts in our understanding of vocation, church, the Christian life, and spirituality. One of those came for me when I was invited to join the staff of The Upper Room to direct a ministry, primarily calling people to a life of prayer, providing direction and resources for practice and growth in prayer—giving structure to a united expression of prayer by readers of The Upper Room magazine around the world.

I told Wilson Weldon, then editor of The Upper Room, that the fact the leadership was inviting me to assume this responsibility showed what a desperate condition the church was in, since I was such a novice in this area of my life.

The responsibility of that job forced me to be more deliberate and disciplined in my own personal life of prayer, and introduced me to a wider dimension of spirituality than I had known.

During those days, I knew no one within the Protestant tradition who was talking about spiritual formation. The Roman Catholics have known the importance of this aspect of Christian growth and have used "formation" language through the centuries. It wasn't long before we at The Upper Room were talking about spiritual formation and seeking to provide resources for a broader expression of spirituality than we had known before.

I became intensely interested in the great devotional classics. The Upper Room had published a collection of booklets, selections from the great spiritual writings of the ages, writers whose names I barely knew and to whose writings I was a stranger: Julian of Norwich, William Law, François Fénelon, Francis of Assisi, Evelyn Underhill, Brother Lawrence, and an array of others. I began a deliberate practice of keeping company with the saints, seeking to immerse myself in the writings of these pathfinders who endured through the centuries, expressing Christian faith in life and becoming classic resources for the Christian pilgrimage.

These saints through their writings share some characteristics in common:

- They passionately sought the Lord.
- They discovered a gracious God.
- They took scripture seriously.
- Jesus was alive in their experience.
- They practiced discipline, at the heart of which was prayer.

- They didn't seek ecstasy but surrender of their will to the Lord.
- They were thirsty for holiness.
- They lived not for themselves but for God and for others.
- They knew joy and peace, transcending all circumstances.

These characteristics and practices are particularly essential for the vocation of ministry. We introduced this subject in chapter 2 when we talked about "practices." All the saints practiced discipline, with prayer at the heart of it.

> The saints have all known there is no way to become a saint quickly. Discipline is essential. Saint Francis de Sales gave direction to be followed throughout our ministry journey...from beginning to end: "We must begin with a strong and constant resolution to give ourselves wholly to God, professing to him, in a tender, loving manner, from the bottom of our hearts, that we intend to be his without reserve, and then we must go back and renew this same resolution." (*A Year with the Saints*, 2)

The purpose of discipline and devotion is to enhance a relationship with Christ, and to cultivate a vivid companionship with him. This is a defining characteristic of the saints: Jesus is alive in their experience. This may be the most distinctive characteristic of the Christian leader. While it is common to translate secular leadership principles into Christian language or jargon, the discipline of keeping Jesus alive, staying in love with God, in your daily experience, is far more compelling.

If Jesus is alive in our experience, we can't evade his most definitive call: "Jesus said to everyone, 'All who want to come after me must say no to themselves, take up their cross daily, and follow me. All who want to save their lives will lose them. But all who lose their lives because of me will save them'" (Luke 9:23-24 CEB).

Jesus's death on the cross and his call to deny ourselves, take up his cross daily, and follow him are at the heart of Christian faith, spirituality, and discipleship. The saints teach us that discipline, in which prayer changes the heart and mind, gives evidence of the cross in our life. When they talked about renunciation, submission, mortification, and surrender, the cross was always in their minds.

Protestant Christians replaced the crucifix in our churches with an empty cross to witness to the empty tomb and Resurrection. But let's be thoughtful; though we know that the death of Jesus without Resurrection could never accomplish our salvation that God provides, we should never ignore or diminish Jesus's passion, suffering, and death. This truth is what led Martin Luther to express his thoughts about Christianity in this clear statement:

> He who is not *crucianus*, if I may coin a word, is not *Christianus*; in other words, he who does not bear his cross is no Christian, for he is not like his Master, Jesus Christ. (*The Joy of the Saints: Spiritual Readings throughout the Year*, introduced and arranged by Robert Llewelyn [Springfield, IL: Templegate Publishers, 1989], 258)

When we appropriate principles of leadership from the secular worlds of competition and conflict, even where the principle of "servant" leadership is emphasized, look for evidence of the cross, and whether the business or political principles are in harmony with Jesus's call to deny ourselves, and his admonition that the "first should be last." When a person comes to your church because they have been given water at a festival on an extremely hot day, help them find the principle of unselfish serving clearly demonstrated in the life of the congregation. Keeping the cross at the center of our awareness always forces us to assess the depth of our discipleship and the degree of our yielding of self to Christ. Luther has a good word for us: "Seek yourself only in Christ and not in yourself; then you will find yourself in him eternally" (*The Joy of the Saints*, 315). The most neglected incarnate principle among Christian leaders is the one most needed in the leader's life: the indwelling Christ. Along with justification by grace though faith, this was Paul's primary emphasis, that the secret core of the Christian life is grounding our being in Christ.

Jesus extended a dual invitation, "Come to me" and "Remain in me." To remain or to abide means to stay with, to dwell. The presence of Christ is not to be experienced only on occasion; the indwelling Christ is to be the shaping power of our lives.

If we are called to be Christian leaders, we must stay aware of the difference between following Christ and being in Christ. Following Jesus is important, but when the Christian way of life is reduced to that, it is limited to a religion of morals and ethics, thus denuding it of its power to transform. To be sure, we are called to follow, to be like Christ, but we can't follow and imitate for long unless we are in Christ, abiding in him.

Staying with Christ requires a dynamic expressed in two characteristics of the saints: first, they believed that obedience was essential; and second, they did not seek ecstasy but surrender to God. These two characteristics can be expressed as *attention* and *abandonment.*

God is constantly calling us to pay attention. In Perry County, Mississippi, where I grew up, we had a quaint but descriptive way of talking about an emerging courtship. Someone would say, "John is paying attention to Mary." Isn't that idiom beautiful? Courtship is a good metaphor for talking about our relationship with God. The Bible suggests that metaphor in various ways. God woos us, courts us, seeking to get our attention—but more thoroughly to get our commitment and our loyal love. God is a jealous God (Josh 24:19).

Only as we pay attention continuously do we stay in touch with our identity and calling. Thomas Merton, the Trappist monk, asked himself the probing question, "Who am I?" and gave a poignant answer, "I am myself, a word spoken by God." He was paying attention. That's what Dietrich Bonhoeffer was doing in a Nazi prison, which he left only in death. Having considered at length whether he was a bold knight of Christian courage that his family and friends and jailers thought him to be, or whether he was just the lonely, caged, fainthearted one that he knew himself to be, he concluded with these thoughts:

Who am I? They mock me, these lonely questions of mine.
Whoever I am, thou knowest, O God, I am thine.

When we pay attention, "Who am I?" gives way to the real human vocational question, "Whose am I?" and there's no equivocation in Bonhoeffer's answer, "Thou knowest, O God, I am thine" (Bonhoeffer, *Letters and Papers from Prison* [New York: Touchstone, 1953/1997], 347–48).

Go back to my introductory story of Saint Patrick. A voice spoke to him: "Return to Ireland, and, preach the gospel." He paid attention. The result? "When I awoke I felt as if I were a slave again—but now God was my Master."

It's not easy to stay at that point of confidence. Most of us are in and out of that conviction. At times we feel deserted and alone. The silence of God haunts, even taunts us. Rare is the person who does not know "dry times," when we simply feel lifeless. I call it the "spiritual blahs." Then there are those "dark nights of the soul" when we cry with the psalmist, "I'm like some wild owl—like some screech owl in the desert" (Ps 102:6 CEB). And yet, we still need to pay attention—always remembering who we are—that we're God's called out, and seek to understand how we are to lead out of that "calling," to be prophet/priest, to be as concerned about being and doing, to seek integrity of performance and identity.

Integrity is where obedience and abandonment apply. We have a right to ask, to seek, and to know the will of God, but once we know it, only one thing is in order: obedience. As noted earlier, it is not our ability to do what God calls us to do but our willingness to respond, to yield, and to attempt that releases God's power.

Peter Cartwright, one of the principal agents God used in the great revival near the beginning of the nineteenth century, clearly demonstrates this truth. He was in the front rank of leadership among the pioneer Methodist preachers of America. He was famous not because of his education or learning; he had little of these. A biographer said, "His great spiritual power and native common sense and shrewdness made him known all over America and in many other lands as well" (James Gilchrist Lawson, *Deeper Experiences of Famous Christians* [Ulrichsville, OH: Barbour Publishing, 2000], 193). Cartwright reminds us, "It must be remembered that many of us early traveling preachers, who entered the wilderness of the West...had little or no education, no books, and no time to read or study them if we could have had them" (Lawson, *Deeper Experiences*, 193).

Almost immediately after his conversion to the faith at age sixteen, he began to sense and wrestle with the "call." He describes his call, and what he labeled "the power from on high" that came when he finally surrendered:

> At last I literally gave up the world, and started, bidding farewell to father and mother, brothers and sisters, and met Brother Lotspeich (the elder preacher/leader) at an appointment in Logan County. He told me I must preach that night. This I had never done; mine was an exhorter's dispensation. I tried to beg off, but he urged me to make the effort. I went out and prayed fervently for aid from heaven. All at once it seemed to me as if I could never preach at all, but I struggled in prayer. At length I asked God, if He had

called me to preach, to give me aid that night, and give me one soul, that is, convert one soul under my preaching, as evidence that I was called to this work.

I went into the house, took my stand, gave out a hymn, sang, and prayed. I rose, gave them the text Isaiah 26:4: "Trust in the Lord for ever, for in the Lord Jehovah is everlasting strength." The Lord gave light, liberty, and power; the congregation was melted into tears. There was present a professed infidel. The word reached his heart by the eternal Spirit. He was powerfully convicted, and, as I believe, soundly converted to God that night and joined the Church, and afterward became a useful member of the same. (Lawson, *Deeper Experiences*, 195–96)

Cartwright was nineteen, and felt his utter inability to preach without power from God. Like Jacob, he wrestled in prayer until he obtained the blessing. He continued to preach with great power until he died at eighty-seven.

Abandonment is the fruit of obedience. All those we would seek to model as Christian leaders were convinced that obedience was essential for their life and growth. We remember that word of Jesus:

> Not everybody who says to me, "Lord, Lord," will get into the kingdom of heaven. Only those who do the will of my Father who is in heaven will enter. On the Judgment Day, many people will say to me, "Lord, Lord, didn't we prophesy in your name and expel demons in your name and do lots of miracles in your name?" Then I'll tell them, "I've never known you. Get away from me, you people who do wrong." (Matt 7:21-23 CEB)

As stated earlier, we do have a responsibility to ask, to seek, and to know the will of God, but once we know it, nothing but obedience will do. The saints of the ages sought to arrive at the place in their relationship to Christ that their one longing was to live and walk in a way that would please God and bring glory to God's name.

Obedience means abandonment. Jean-Pierre de Caussade wrote to one who depended upon his spiritual guidance that abandonment to God "is, of all practices, the most divine."

> Your way of acting in times of trouble and distress gives me great pleasure. To be submissive, to abandon yourself entirely without reserve, to be content with being discontented for as long as God wills or permits, will make you advance more in one day than you would in a hundred days spent in sweetness and consolation. Your total abandonment to God, practiced in a spirit of confidence, and of union with Jesus Christ doing always the will of his father, is, of all practices, the most divine. (*The Joy of the Saints*, 101)

Our spiritual formation as Christian leaders is a dynamic process, a growing willingness, or even a willingness to be made willing, to say yes to God every day in every way possible—no matter what the circumstances may be. The more we pay attention to God, the more aware we will become of the yet-to-be redeemed areas of our life—and the more we will need to abandon ourselves to the transforming power of the indwelling Christ.

Jesus made clear how essential abandonment is when he taught us to pray "Thy will be done." There are two common ways we pray this prayer. Sometimes, we wrestle against God.

We receive intimations of something God wants us to do—some call—and we wrestle against God because we are not sure we want to respond. Or sometimes we come face to face with an issue requiring God's justice and holiness—and we resist. We don't want to do it.

But there's also another kind of wrestling. It's not wrestling against God; it's a matter of wrestling with God against that which opposes God's will. It really becomes a matter of spiritual warfare, though we must be very careful not to confuse our interpretation of God's will with a calling to deliver God's punitive wrath. We sense that there are forces within our world opposed to God's will: sickness, hate and meanness, narrowness of spirit, fear, lethargy, prejudice, and ill will. This wrestling leads to our resistance toward the forces of darkness—and sometimes we wrestle against the evil one. We set ourselves against all such forces and to them we cry, "God's will be done on earth as it is in heaven."

As a form of abandonment, sometimes when we pray, "Thy will be done," it is a declaration of submission in which we confess that we do not know what is best but we want God's will. We struggle, we wrestle, we stay in the presence of the Lord until our hearts are made tender, and we're ready to trust God and surrender our will.

My favorite story about Lourdes has to do with an old priest at that famous healing center who was asked one time by a newspaper reporter to describe the most impressive miracle he'd ever seen there. The reporter expected him to talk about the amazing recovery of someone who had come to Lourdes ill and walked away well. "Not at all," the old priest said, "if you want to know the greatest miracle that I have ever seen at Lourdes, it is the look of radiant resignation on the face of those who turn away unhealed!" That's abandonment! "Thy will be done" as a declaration of submission, confessing that all we want is God's will—because we know that it is best for us.

There are three seeds that, when planted in the soil of obedience, produce the fruit of God's will in our lives: first, scripture study; second, conferencing (deliberately and honestly sharing with godly persons for edification and discerning God's will and guidance); and third, divine conviction wrought by the Holy Spirit.

In the divine school of obedience, we know there is a textbook: scripture. We know there is a model to imitate: Jesus. We also know and have experienced the way the Holy Spirit will plant a deep, deep conviction within our lives, calling us to go in a particular direction.

Ezekiel, our example of the prophet/priest, brings attention and abandonment together.

> Then he said to me: Human one, eat this thing that you've found. Eat this scroll and go, speak to the house of Israel. So I opened my mouth, and he fed me the scroll. He said to me: Human one, feed your belly and fill your stomach with this scroll that I give you. So I ate it, and in my mouth it became as sweet as honey. (Ezek 3:1-3 CEB)

The saints saturated themselves in scripture. The more fully we become one with God's Word, the more authentic our leadership will be Christian. In addition to prayer, searching the scripture is a means of grace and a distinctive leadership principle for Christians.

The fundamental meaning of *disciple*, which Christian leaders are to model, is the learner or pupil. Jesus was called rabbi because rabbis are teachers. The Great Rabbi himself called us to "put on my yoke, and learn from me" (Matt 11:29 CEB). The prophet Hosea in the eighth century was the first leader in scripture to teach us that we are to love God with our hearts and know God with our minds. Our primary source for that knowledge about God is the library of sixty-six books in the Christian Bible.

John Wesley was an extremely well-read scholar. Yet, on more than one occasion, he referred to himself as "a man of one book." Perhaps the most significant example of that self-identification is in the preface to his sermons. He writes autobiographically, portraying himself as a seeker after truth:

> I am a spirit come from God, and returning to God: just hovering over the great gulf; till, a few moments hence, I am no more seen; I drop into an unchangeable eternity! I want to know one thing—the way to heaven; how to land safe on the other shore. God himself has condescended to teach the way; for this very end He came from heaven. He hath written it down in a book. O give me that book! At any price, give me the book of God! I have it: here is knowledge enough for me. Let me be *homo unibus libri* (man of one book). (Albert Outler and Richard Heitzenreter, eds., *John Wesley's Sermons: An Anthology* [Nashville: Abingdon, 1991], 9)

As we become one with God's Word, what we say must be matched by how we live—because character and calling can't be separated.

Bonhoeffer in prison asked the question, "Who am I?" This question means that the formation of a Christian leader is a dynamic process in which we seek more and more to respond recklessly to that primal question, "Who am I?"

Pretension, then, is a distraction to vital spirituality and integrity in leadership. Likewise, imitation is a distraction. To project or to seek to fit into a standardized pattern of spirituality or leadership is to miss the meaning of God's gracious creativity that made each one of us a "unique unrepeatable miracle of God."

The purpose of discipline and formation is not to make us all carbon copies of some pre-determined model of a saint, or a carbon copy of some great leader, but rather to call forth the rich diversity of gifts within us, and to empower the expression of those gifts. Imitation is deadly.

Bernard Shaw was an agnostic, but carried on a correspondence for many years with a cloistered nun. It is one of the strangest relationships in history, but also one of the most intriguing and beautiful. Here is Shaw, the intellectual, the playwright, a man of the world, a man of considerable wealth; and the nun, cloistered, who gave up worldly possessions, to pursue a life of work and prayer. In one of his letters to her, he wrote, "The next time I'm in your neighborhood, I will peer through the bars of your cell to see the freedom on the other side" (quoted by Mark Trotter, in a sermon titled "Need Any Water?" preached at the First United Methodist Church, San Diego, CA, March 19, 1995).

Shaw knew and was expressing what freedom is all about; the freedom, the joyous freedom, that comes only through the dynamic of attention and abandonment, enabling us to be who God created us to be.

Leaders Are to Be Saints

We considered four specific characteristics of the saints:

- They practiced spiritual discipline, with prayer at its center.
- Jesus was alive in their experience.
- They believed obedience was essential.
- They did not seek ecstasy but surrender to God.

We gave meaning to obedience and surrender through the concepts of attention and abandonment. We contend that as leaders who are prophet/priests we must become one with God's Word; the saints saturated themselves in and took scripture seriously.

To frame this chapter around lessons from the saints is at least a suggestion that leaders are to be saints. One of my mentors, Douglas Steere, provides the definition I am using when I make that suggestion.

> He is an "apostle," or if you like, a "saint"...only as whatever capacities he possesses are wholly open to use for the purposes of God. He is a saint by reason of the totality of his abandonment to God....A saint is "just one human being released from the love of self and enslaved by the love of God," and rejoices in it. (*On Beginning from Within* [New York: Harper & Brothers, 1943], 33, 35)

CHAPTER 4

What Is Good Ministry?

In *On Not Knowing How to Live*, Alan Wheelis, a practicing psychoanalyst in San Francisco, describes a philosophy of life by using the "Big Top" of the circus tent as an analogy.

> Stay with the main show.... Do not be drawn off into side shows and diversions... do only what you are most solemnly charged to do.... There in the Big Top, a man is hanging by his teeth, twisting, spinning, spotlights playing over him, the drums beginning to roll. He's going to fall and nothing can be done—no net—but in the moments remaining he may yet achieve something remarkable, some glittering stunt, a movement, perhaps of breath taking beauty.... Any turning away to watch the dancing bears is a betrayal of the dangling man... hold fast, stay with him. (New York: Harper and Row, 1975)

This advice can be easily perceived in the Christian faith, and especially by pastors and Christian leaders. There are religious sideshows offered with enticing attractions all around us—and it will always be the case—the religious versions of dancing bears, stripteases, and peepshows. These would divert our attention. They are the sideshows. They come and they go.

And then there is the main show. What is it? What is the main show that needs to be played out under the big top of the ministry to which we are called? So we ask, "What is good ministry?" Or "What is it that makes a truly good minister?" There is a sense in which this entire book is seeking to answer that, but here I narrow the focus.

A list comes quickly to our minds when we think of the qualities we would hope for in a minister, and the skills essential for the practice of ministry. The following would probably appear on the list any of us would make:

- an experience of salvation that is readily witnessed
- a clear sense of call
- a love of God and a love of people
- a working knowledge of scripture, church history, and theological thought expressed through an active intelligence
- an ongoing practice of the disciplines that grows in holiness and spiritual maturity

The list would certainly include a litany of skills required for effective ministry. In one way or another, in what congregations always say they want in a minister these would be registered:

- a leader who can inspire confidence
- a person who can preach
- a person who loves people and demonstrates pastoral concern

- a "spiritual leader," with moral and ethical integrity whose character is not questioned

The list would be long and nuanced in many different ways, according to our own experience and bias. It would clearly demonstrate there is a monumental array of expectations, leading any candidate for ministry to honestly exclaim, "Woe is me; who is worthy and could ever be adequate for such a calling?"

Bedrock Grounding in God

Careful reflection and studies of experienced ministers and congregational lay leaders confirm that the core dynamic out of which good ministry grows is a bedrock grounding in God. We keep this grounding alive by recognizing, cultivating awareness of, and giving expression to the indwelling Christ.[1] Unless we find and cultivate this primary grounding, we will never be competent, effective ministers and leaders, and those we seek to lead will be the big losers. Roberta Bondi describes the failure to cultivate this grounding:

> Unconsciously or consciously, they will do the things in their churches that they think they need to affirm their own being and give them value in their own eyes, and they will not do the things that threaten that value given by others. They may not be able to tell the difference between the structures and pronouncements of church and the God they profess to serve.

---

1. In my book *Alive in Christ*, this is my expression of the dynamic process of spiritual formation (Nashville: Abingdon, 1982).

Chapter 4

As though that is not enough to convince us of the destructive impact of not being grounded in God, Bondi states the case with more devastating consequences:

> They may be authoritarian, inauthentic, threatened not only by new social patterns but also by new theological approaches, dismissive of the Christian tradition, or rigid with respect to it. They may be wishy-washy, disdainful, lazy, self-deceptive, sexually predatory, financially crooked, unable to set priorities, and ultimately burned out.

Then she pictures the alternative:

> On the other hand, if they are sure in the depths of their being that their center rests in God, and they know how to keep in constant awareness of it, those same ministers can truly grow into the right kind of love for the people they serve. They will not be afraid of the elderly, the sick, the handicapped, or the dying, and they will insist on a place for them in their congregations. They will care about the poor, they will see folks as they really are and not be judgmental because they will be very sure that God loves all the congregation infinitely, as God loves the ministers themselves, and they will communicate that love convincingly. They will be anxious to drink deeply of our common Christian resources in scripture, tradition, and modern theology, and they will be hungry to find ways to share with their congregations in the clearest possible manner the practical, saving insights of those resources. (Roberta C. Bondi, "Centered in God," from *A Collection of Portraits and Essays about Good Ministry*, Pulpit and Pew and the Fund for Theological Education, Duke University Divinity School, 2003)

Sprouting from bedrock grounding in God, and nourished by disciplines for spiritual formation, good ministry will wed prophetic imagination and intention with pastoral compassion and attention.

Prophetic Imagination

While I was president of Asbury Theological Seminary, we had a controversy over the way the American flag and other symbols were used in our places of worship and common areas. On March 19, 2003, the United States, along with coalition forces primarily from the United Kingdom, initiated war on Iraq. The case for war was built primarily on the idea that Iraq, under dictator Saddam Hussein, possessed or was in the process of building weapons of mass destruction.

We were having a community dinner in the commons the week after the war started. Some students, not responsible for decoration, placed a few small American flags in the center of every table. We were in the midst of Lent; Easter was coming in April. Other students, not responsible for decorations, thinking them not appropriate at the time in that place, removed the flags.

Those who had placed the flags were a bit short of outraged. Lines were clearly drawn between supporters and opponents of the war in Iraq, and war in general.

As president of the seminary, I felt this was a pregnant teaching moment. In my prayer time one morning before a crucial gathering of the community for worship, that same week, when it was apparent to me that I needed to speak to the controversy, which was also being discussed in the public press, the Spirit gave me the principle: prophetic intention must be wed to pastoral attention.

This kind of revelation doesn't happen often to me, but with that concept the Spirit had my attention. I prayed and pondered, wondering: Where had the word come from and what was its relevance? Our community swirled in controversy. The newspapers and radio reported the issue unfairly; persons with deeply held views and commitments were finding it hard to live together. I reminded our community that how we lived together in a community of differing opinions and commitments related to the awful, painful war through which we were going, how we related to one another when feelings and emotions were so raw and convictions so strong, how we processed ideas, information, the message of scripture, our understanding of vocation—all of this provided perhaps the most poignant teaching moment our students would have during their time there.

Over the next few weeks some of our professors led groups in response, and I informed the students that I would give my assistant the word that their appointments with me during the next few weeks to share about the war would be given priority.

The questions were no longer hypothetical. How do we wrestle theologically with the complexities of world events? How do we grapple with what it means to be a pastor? How do we preach to people when issues are confusing and divisive? How do we serve the prophetic role, being faithful to God, speaking to the people for God, without being politically partisan? How do we live in a community that is a cameo of the diversity of God's church?

The Wedding of the Prophetic and Pastoral

Chapter 2 describes the shape of vocational leadership as that of prophet/priest, which when faithfully expressed shows people that God's representative has been among them. The primary function of the prophet/priest is twofold: speaking to the people for God and speaking to God for the people. I suggested this dynamic as prophetic intention and pastoral attention.

So now the dynamic in the word the Spirit gave me during that crisis is expanded. Prophetic imagination and intention must be wed to pastoral compassion and attention. It is clear from the formula (speaking to) that the prophetic imagination and intention of good ministry has to do primarily with the proclamation of the Word. It is the Word that creates and shapes the church. Karl Barth expressed this basic truth:

> The community is created and confronted by the Word of God. It is *communio sanctorium*, the community of saints, because it is *congregation fidelium*, the gathering of the faithful. As such, it is *coniuratio testium*, the confederation of witnesses who may and must speak because they believe. (Karl Barth, *Evangelical Theology: An Introduction*, trans. Grover Foley [Grand Rapids: Eerdmans, 1963], 38)

There is a sense in which a person may have great ministry skills, and be a person of virtue and Spirit-life, but if she or he can't proclaim the Word, good ministry doesn't happen. To have prophetic imagination and exercise prophetic intention, the Word of God must dwell in us richly. It is out of what Rebecca Chop calls "a Word-drenched community" that faith is nourished and prophetic witness is made.

The prophetic imagination sees God's love active in the world. Martha Nussbaum speaks about imagination in relation to liberal education. She calls it "narrative imagination." She means by this imaginations so formed that other ways of being can be seen (Martha C. Nussbaum, "The Narrative Imagination," *Cultivating Humanity: A Classic Defense of Reform in Liberal Education* [Cambridge, MA: Harvard University Press, 1997], 85–112).

Christian leaders need Christian narrative imagination. We see an example of this in the Beatitudes. The Beatitudes are a statement of how the Christian is to see the world...not as it is but as it should be.

Prophetic intention calls us to live in light of how the world might be or should be; to live as though the Kingdom had already come, thus we approximate in the earthly order that which is already present in God's kingdom.

Good ministry, or the person who would be a truly good minister, weds prophetic imagination and intention with pastoral compassion and attention. Proclamation of the Word is essential for this vision of how things are and how they should be. Soul care (pastoral compassion) joins proclamation as the most important components of good ministry.

What Is Good Ministry?

In his biography of Mother Teresa, Malcolm Muggeridge provides a dramatic demonstration of pastoral attention. The biography grew out of a television film project. For the purpose of filming, they accompanied Mother Teresa to the Home for the Dying, where lepers and unwanted children filled the place. Muggeridge said he went through three phases in his thinking and feeling about all he was seeing. The first was horror mixed with pity; the second compassion, pure and simple; and the third, reaching far beyond compassion to something he had never experienced before,

> an awareness that these dying and derelict men and women, these lepers with stumps instead of hands, these unwanted children, were not pitiable, repulsive or forlorn, but rather dear and delightful; as it might be, friends of long standing, brothers and sisters. How is it to be explained—the very heart and mystery of the Christian faith? To soothe those battered old heads, to grasp those poor stumps, to take in one's arms those children consigned to dustbins, because it is [Jesus's] head, as they are His stumps and His children, of whom He said that whosoever received one such child in His name received Him. (Muggeridge, *Something Beautiful for God*, quoted in Reuben P. Job and Norman Shawchuck, *A Guide to Prayer for Ministers and Other Servants* [Nashville: The Upper Room, 1983], 233)

This dramatic story serves only to underscore the importance of what may be seen mundane in day-to-day ministry—pastoral attention to

- the growing population of the elderly
- working single mothers who are strained to a

breaking point as they desperately care for their children

- those who have been traumatized by sexual abuse and assault, and feel the church doesn't care, much less understand
- the wealthy who know success but whose lives are empty, barren of significance
- the postmodern twenty- and thirty-something adults who welcome experience and relationship but are not very impressed with our rational arguments
- the ethnically and economically marginalized who need a voice and a break

Prophetic imagination and intention must be wed to pastoral compassion and attention, especially when people from every walk of life are looking for a leader to speak to God for them.

Making Secure and Shaking Up

By the 1980s, Lyle Schaller observed that ministry, once a "high status, low stress" vocation, is just the opposite: "high stress and low status." Why? Clergy have a double calling, both to secure and to shake people up. They need to be prophetic and pastoral at the same time. Most people want ministers to stabilize their lives, to keep them from being shaken. Many participants come to church to find and achieve stability. They don't want to be shaken. They want to be secured. Yet, ministers, exercising "good ministry," also shake people up. Prophetic intention and pastoral attention is called for. Many years ago, there was a distinguished pastor at First United Methodist Church in Evanston, Illinois. This church was known for its social prophetic witness. Ernest Fremont Tittle, the minister, was known across the Methodist connection as a great battler for human rights. Naturally, he upset a lot of people because of his strong stands. However, though most of the congregation were far more conservative than he, he lost very few members from his congregation, which was of great size and national repute.

Along the way, a reporter wrote a story about Pastor Tittle and the church. He interviewed members, and asked why all the members seemed so intensely loyal to their pastor. The answer was unanimous. Ernest Tittle loved his people, deeply. He was always there for them, never personally critical, always ready to visit the hospital, to receive them in counseling, to marry the young and caringly bury the dead. His door was always open to those who wished to visit in order to debate the issues, and they always left feeling they had been heard.

This is a powerful witness about prophetic intention and pastoral attention. It is a great lesson to be learned by all, pastors and others, about good ministry. We can be prophetic. We can take strong stands on social issues, if people know we love them, that we will not only listen to them but will listen with integrity and pastoral concern. Many issues are controversial, with room for earnest opinions on both sides. We can stand firmly on our beliefs, yet listen to and honor the rights of those who see things differently. It is important to examine our own hearts to be sure we ourselves are not holding our own positions out of mixed motives, some of them not so worthy.

I don't know why and how, along with twenty-three hundred others, I received an invitation to attend the March 2, 2018, funeral service of Billy Graham, the best-known and most loved and trusted evangelical leader during the past century. He appeared on the Gallup Poll's list of the "10 Most Admired Men in the World" over sixty times. When asked how he would like to be remembered, he answered, "As a preacher of the gospel of Jesus Christ."

He was criticized by some for not "being prophetic enough." Yet when I was involved in the civil rights struggle in Mississippi in the mid-1960s, I was encouraged by the fact that he would not preach in an evangelistic crusade unless it was open to all people, regardless of race. Not only so, I often found myself defending my prophetic preaching by referring to Billy Graham and his stand on racial inclusion.

As I participated in the worship service honoring this faithful servant, I reflected on my own sixty years of ministry. I was smitten by an awareness that, whether as a prophet or priest, my reward has been the satisfaction that comes from knowing I am being faithful to God's calling. I know my obedience to the gospel might be measured by the degree of tension and conflict it has generated. Also, the effectiveness might be measured by how, in my obedience, I have sought to be pastoral, aware, and appreciative of "the sense of the faithful."

The Sense of the Faithful

Good ministry always pays attention to the sense of the faithful. I get the phrase from John Henry Cardinal Newman. As a priest, in 1859, he wrote an article for a Roman Catholic periodical, *The Rambler*, of which he was the editor. The article caused such a controversy, and the bishops of the church were so upset they asked him to resign, so he did. He later became a cardinal.

Newman was affirming the critical role of the laity of the church. He carried his affirmation to the point of insisting that the consensus of the faithful may preserve important doctrines even when the bishops fail.

This was a revolutionary notion, akin to Martin Luther's "justification by grace though faith." This elevated view of the laity got little traction in the wider Roman Catholic Church until the Second Vatican Council, where it became a big issue, and Newman's article played a significant role in the discussion.

Newman made the case that there is lodged in the church—the body of Christ comprising primarily laity—a depository of profound practical theological wisdom. If the Roman Catholic Church can positively entertain that notion, how much more should we be able to do so as Protestants who champion the priesthood of all believers?

Good ministry belongs to the whole people of God, and those who are ordained as leaders must not only acknowledge this but must lead in ordering the life of the congregation to this end.

CHAPTER 5

The Persons We Are and the Institutions We Serve

In chapter 2, we considered the shape of our vocation in terms of prophet/priest, the persons we are as we live vocationally. That dynamic can't be isolated from the institutions we serve.

There is no question about it: leaders shape in significant ways the institutions they serve. It is sobering to consider the sense in which an organization takes on the characteristics of its leader or leaders. For that reason, more often than not, the quality and effectiveness of an organization is in large part attributed to those who lead it.

Recognizing this makes it imperative for those whose vocation is Christian leadership to always be mindful of the identity, ethos, and mission of the institutions they serve. This is especially true of the local congregation. Having served as the president of a seminary and as lead executive for a spiritual formation agency, I can witness to the fact that other institutionalized forms of ministry are also shaped significantly by the leader. Even so, the focus here is on leadership of

Chapter 5

a congregation, which is a community with memory and imagination.

A Community of Memory

Memory is one of our most important capacities. It is a blessed gift. James M. Barrie said, "God gave us memory so that we might have roses in December." But it is more than recalling beauty. Memory gives us a sense of meaning. We are who we are because of memory. When we begin to lose memory, we become disconnected from life. Amnesia, often brought about by some shattering, life-threatening experience, is the loss of memory and a disconnection from life.

My wife and I are presently living in a retirement village that has the whole range of life care. There is a section for persons with Alzheimer's, a degenerative brain disease. This is an extreme expression of amnesia. Some of our friends who are living independently have spouses who are living in the Alzheimer's section. I can't imagine anything more emotionally painful—to have a husband or a wife with whom you have shared forty years of marriage now not know who you are. Loss of memory disconnects one from life.

We are who we are and the church is who it is because of memory. Memory is not only the ongoing source of life for the Christian community, how memory functions in our communal life shapes how life is ordered and expressed. Any degree of amnesia distorts; total amnesia destroys. Memory keeps the Christian community alive. The Christian faith and its liveliness in the world as a redemptive community is dependent in large part upon its "living memory" of God's singular act of grace and generosity in Jesus, his Son. If that memory is lost, if that memory does not shape our present life and create and empower a distinctive community, what the New Testament calls *koinonia*, then the church cannot be sustained.

As leaders we not only have a fiscal, administrative, and the traditional pastoral responsibility, we are responsible for the tradition, the ethos, the mission of our congregations, ministries, or institutions we serve. As a leader, I must be constantly asking, "What is it that we hold in memory and carry forward in our life"?

Pastors of independent churches, or pastors involved in new church plants, have a challenging responsibility with respect to memory. As pastors and leaders shaping the tradition, casting the vision, and laying the foundation, it is crucial to communicate a solid biblical basis for the nature of the church as catholic (universal) and apostolic. The opportunity is to connect a new, freshly formed congregation to the universal body of Christ.

If a pastor serves an independent congregation, make sure that leaders and participants are not lone rangers in the Christian world, separated from what God has done in raising up peoples who may have different identities and structures, but have been raised up to share in God's kingdom enterprise, and always bring God glory. At the core of your calling is to contend for, and even defend, "the faith once and for all delivered to the saints." Some may interpret "the faith once and for all" differently than I; yet, for myself, I can't be a responsible leader as a pastor, as a leader in theological education or in spiritual formation without that community of memory sustaining a vital part of my pastoral attention.

And so there is no Christian tradition to remember that does not recall a personal relationship with Jesus Christ. Check it out in scripture and Christian history. Check it out in the history of the community you serve as you consider the question: "What is it that we hold in our memory and carry forward in our life that gives us our unique identity and shapes our mission?" If the dynamic, renewing presence and power of Jesus Christ is not present, Christian community diminishes and eventually dies.

Some leaders seek to be all things to all persons until they forget who they are; some leaders dilute the claims of the gospel and the demands of discipleship in order to attract more people. There is the danger of being so broad in what we publicly offer that we then find it impossible to cultivate the depth of commitment and spirituality that should characterize Christian community.

Relevance is important. It's not enough to know theology and scripture abstractly. If we are faithful shepherds for the people to God, do we know their unique needs and problems? Are we listening to the soundtracks of our age: the longings, the hurts, the aspirations? Are we communicating in media and on platforms where the questions are actually being asked?

We should be relevant, but we must be grounded. We can be so laser focused on the culture that our memory is too loosely held. We can so identify with the people around us that we forget we are ambassadors of Christ's kingdom. When we do this we not only fail our mission as Christ followers, we fail the people we are called to serve. Only the story of Christ among us answers the deepest human longing and need. The bottom line of that story is there is no Christian tradition apart from a personal relationship with Jesus Christ. That memory must be kept alive to shape our vision and mission.

A Community of Imagination

A community of memory also cultivates a community of imagination. Memory without imagination turns many would-be leaders into reactionaries. Remember that word about Father Molloy? "You were a part of and related to a great past, and yet you were so close to many of us. You believed in the joy of life.... You faced life as it is, and as it changes."

Marshall McLuhan, author of *The Medium Is the Message*, talked about our looking at culture through a rearview mirror. He also described technological sleepwalking. "When technologies are created and absorbed quickly into culture, we tend to sleepwalk. We move about culture in a stupor, not understanding that technologies have systemic effects. Critics can't afford to be sleepwalkers" (Douglas Groothuis, "The Soul in Cyberspace: The Ethical Issues," *Discernment* [Spring 1998]: 2).

One way to inhibit the stupor from rapid cultural change driven by technology is to become a community of imagination. We read and understand the signs of the times in order to be influential in what we do in service for Christ. There is a sense in which every pastoral leader should be a cultural anthropologist—able to analyze, understand, and critique the forces that are shaping the lives of people around us.

We need to be both "in the Book" and "in the community"—that is, steeped in Christian theology and ethics, and deeply engaged with the people we serve. Sure, people are facing opportunities, conveniences, addictions, and temptations vastly different and more widely transmitted and commercialized than during the days of our grandparents' generation. The addictions and temptations mediated by digital technologies seem new or more potent, yet they are versions of the human condition that has caused such pain and suffering since the beginning. The Christian leader is not surprised by new ways to exploit our human weaknesses and selfish appetites.

John Gardiner, in his book on leadership, talks about members of institutions getting into a "trance of non-renewal," getting so used to flaws and limitations that they look right past them; they get used to living with them. Members of congregations experience that. Perhaps worse, not only do they get used to the flaws and limitations, they fail to see opportunities. Mark Trotter says not only do churches experience a "trance of non-renewal," they have their "chant of non-renewal." There are multiple versions of it: "We never did it that way." "It won't work here." "We are too small to take on anything that big." "The older members won't like it." Opportunity comes and they don't even see it. The door to a more significant and missional future opens and they don't walk through, thus missing contributing redemptively to their community.

To sustain memory and imagination in the community, we seek a balance between conservation and vision. The balancing of these together is an especially weighty matter because of the religious and political climate emerging in the Western world. At no time in my ministry have I seen such an expansive expression of division and hostility as today—in the political arena, yes, but also in the church. Rhetoric in the public media, particularly on television, has overtones of accusation and anger. Secular leaders, but also Christian leaders, have feelings of persecution and harassment. They feel threatened and discounted. The anger and hostility may be understandable, but it is toxic and more harmful to our spiritual wholeness than the causes of the frustration are.

We have long observed that secularism is marked by the inability of persons shaped by scientific materialism to believe in and accept God's grace or love. But overshadowing intellectual doubt is an emerging phenomenon of "hyper-credulity," that is, the ability and willingness to believe anything. When this propensity to believe anything presented in the dress of spirituality is connected with an exaggerated notion of inclusivity, the memory and imagination of the Christian community is diluted until a congregation and its leader no longer make disciples of Jesus for the transformation of the world.

While seeking the balance between the ancient and the future, Christian communities must present compelling and imaginative new versions of a distinctively Christian faith. I register three areas, which increasingly demand the leader's attention and imagination.

First, worship. Many worship scholars think that we've been moving through a worship reformation since the 1970s.

So leaders should guide their congregations to ask, in an ongoing way, questions like these:

- Why are there so many members of our churches who are not attending worship faithfully?
- Why does our worship not attract the forty-year-old adult and those younger?
- Is our worship style and language understandable and attractive only to those who have a Christian history?
- What about our music? Have we made an idol of the organ, the worship band, or a particular style of music?
- Have we, perhaps not intentionally but by default, become elitist in our worship, bound by habits long refined and too long unquestioned; habits that make little sense and have little attraction to secular persons who are not schooled in our ways?
- Do we see our worship as our witness? As a primary expression of evangelism?

Questioning in this fashion is essential because nothing is more integral to what we are about as Christians than worship. We must constantly assess the integrity and vitality of the worship life of our congregations.

Along with worship, evangelism demands our attention as we seek to keep alive a community of memory and imagination.

Cultural anthropology is relevant here. I knew the world was changing when I saw a magnificent Muslim mosque just off the freeway in Birmingham, Alabama. Change was further confirmed when shortly thereafter my seatmate on an airline flight was a Muslim PhD student from Mississippi State University in Starkville, Mississippi. Starkville has a population of less than twenty-five thousand and is in one of the most rural areas of the state. In our conversation, I learned they have a small mosque in Starkville, and there is the possibility that the national Muslim leadership will soon provide them an imam.

Not only are we not a Christian nation, we are a nation that no longer considers the Christian faith as a primary maker of our national life. Evangelism in such a context demands serious attention to apologetics. Given postmodernity (which rejects scientific materialism), the rising tide of generic spirituality, and the loss of Christian memory, we can't depend on "four spiritual laws," or any mechanistic system of reason to provide an adequate apologetic for human experience.

As leaders we need to keep asking ourselves and our congregations:

- Do we want to know the people within our reach?
- Do we love them and want them in our worship?
- Are we willing for our church to become their church?
- Are we willing to go where they are and engage them on their turf?
- Are we willing to spend time with them—identify with them and show genuine compassion?

Worship and evangelism are affected by the loss of the church's privileged position in Western society. With rare exception, we live in a multicultural, multireligious community. The preferential treatment Christians expected from culture and government is long past; Christendom is gone. Eventually, the church and every other religious community may no longer have tax-exempt status. Can we be imaginative enough, and loyal enough to God's kingdom, to grasp the loss of preferential treatment as an advantage? Richard Foster explains:

> Instead of the Church desperately trying to elbow her way up to the tables of power, we can instead turn our attention to becoming, by our life and witness, an alternative voice to the madness around us. Since, in Christ we have been reborn into the new reality of the kingdom of God, we can become ambassadors of peace in the midst of a violent world, models of civility and grace in the midst of a competitive society, conveyors of faith and hope in the midst of a cynical culture, and the embodiment of agape love to all peoples in the midst of an adversarial society. ("A Pastoral Letter from Richard Foster," *Renovare* [November 1999])

We must ground everything we do in the awareness that we live in an apostolic situation where Christian experience, Christian memory, and a Christian vocabulary are not a part of our culture. We must recognize that, for the most part, there is less connective tissue between Christian language or symbol and secular culture or many other religious cultures. We've been here before. We are far from the setting of the primitive church of the New Testament and the centuries following. So we must remember the work of the Holy Spirit as the early church expanded, and anticipate with vision and imagination what God can provide to shape the institutions we serve.

Chapter 6

The Preacher and Preaching

A pastor is trusted with the awesome responsibility of preaching the gospel. That trust can affect a pastor's ego. Bishop Gerald Kennedy often told about a bishop in the Church of England, who observed that a sermon is "something a clergy person will cross a continent to deliver, but will not walk across the street to hear." Yet, when we get beyond our egos and our yet unredeemed arrogance, we know that proclamation of the gospel (*kerygma*) is a responsibility infused with the humility of speaking to the people for God. Will Willimon provides a helpful perspective: "We preachers are witnesses, nothing more, tethered to an event we do not control.... We are witnesses whose significance is the event to which we bear witness. We are spear carriers for the risen Christ's retake of the world.... Wonder of wonders, Christ makes his appeal through us."

Every weekend we *witness* and we have a dramatic story to tell. Consider a bizarre event that took place in Patterson, California. It made news across the country in 1986.

Fifteen-year-old Felipe Garza Jr. seemed to be in perfect health, but his girlfriend, Donna Ashlock, had an enlarged heart and needed a transplant. Meanwhile, Felipe told his mother he was going to die, and he wanted Donna to have his heart. His mother was concerned by the intensity of Felipe's feelings, but forgot about it in a couple of days. Two weeks later, Felipe died and she remembered Felipe's sharing, and his death wish was realized; his heart was transplanted to Donna ("Felipe Garza Could Not Win Donna Ashlock's Love but He Gave Her His Heart," https://people.com/archive/felipe-garza-could-not-win-donna-ashlocks-love-but-he-gave-her-his-heart-vol-25-no-4/).

The doctors were puzzled. Though apparently outstandingly healthy, Felipe had awakened with a pain on the left side of his head, was losing breath, and couldn't walk. His brain died with the bursting of a blood vessel. Though he remained technically alive, the family decided to let the physician remove life support so that Felipe's heart could be given to Donna, and his kidneys and eyes to others in need of those organs. We know that the death wish and love are very powerful. Those two enormous powers mysteriously came together in Felipe.

After reading that story, I thought a lot about Donna. She knows literally what it means to be alive because of love, the gift of life from another person. I have often wondered how she talked about that experience. As preachers, every Sunday we tell a story just as dramatic. The letter writer, John, certainly thought so.

> We announce to you what existed from the beginning, what we have heard, what we have seen with our eyes, what we have seen and our hands handled, about the word of life. The life was revealed, and we have seen, and we testify and announce to you the eternal life that was with the Father and was revealed to us. What we have seen and heard, we also announce it to you so that you can have fellowship with us. Our fellowship is with the Father and with his Son, Jesus Christ. We are writing these things so that our joy can be complete. (1 John 1:1-4 CEB)

John's letter goes on to talk about the light that illumines our darkness, about the love of Christ on the cross—his heart for our hearts—forgiving all our sins, and cleansing us from all unrighteousness. Is anything more important than that?

We do hold, as Paul said, "the treasure in dirty and clumsy hands" (2 Cor 4:7, author's paraphrase), nevertheless, we do hold it! Of course, this "awesome power belongs to God and doesn't come from us" (2 Cor 4:7), so "we preach about Jesus Christ as Lord" (2 Cor 4:5).

We preach! Preaching is a kind of heart transplant in a sense that is profoundly real: life and light are transmitted in the message the preacher is called to share. And then people experience *metanoia*, which means God can bring a "change of hearts and lives."

Our Primary Task as Pastors

Since the Lord first called me to speak to the people for God, I am driven by the conviction that proclamation is the core expression of a Christian leader's calling. Since it is that important, I work hard at cultivating the art, being rather disciplined in the practice of preaching. It may be presumptuous to write about it as a practitioner, because working preachers tend to be critical of other preaching, but for the most part they are gracious and generous when they are mutually accountable in their personal relationships. Preachers operate in the arena where love and forgiveness are the most desperate needs of the persons who hear us. We serve as priests, mediating those precious needs.

That does not mean a preacher can presume on the grace of the listeners. To the contrary, too many preachers make that mistake weekly. Undisciplined in their study and personal devotional life, they come to that crucial hour of worship on the weekend, not as someone "ashamed but is one who interprets the message of truth correctly" (2 Tim 2:15 CEB); not as slovenly workers, unprepared, insensitive to the momentousness of the hour, the sacredness of the task, and the potential of being used by God in his miracle of saving people by the "foolishness of preaching" (1 Cor 1:21). So they handle holy things with dirty and clumsy hands.

To speak on preaching in this fashion has forced reflection, which should be an ongoing exercise for the preacher. Most of us, including preachers, are not engaged in reflective self-examination, thus we fail to teach the people we lead to be reflective. Do you regularly sit down with yourself, perhaps for just an hour, and look at the way you exercise your primary calling to preach? Can you hold that up honestly before the Lord, and examine it in light of your total vocation as a person called by God and set apart by the church, a calling to preach the glorious, transforming gospel?

As I make the claim not to presume on your grace, I do not make a claim to originality, and I feel in good company. C. S. Lewis said originality is not the prerogative of us creatures, but is a gift belonging only to God. That does not mean we can't be creative; originality and creativity are not the same. Preaching should be a creative act in which God and the preacher share: speaking for the people and speaking for God.

Though I am not original, I've never been happier or more fulfilled than at 12:30 p.m. on a given Sunday when driving home from worship, with the indescribable feeling that I have been faithful to my calling, have given my best, and thus am pleased to leave it on the altar of God as an offering, confident that in leaving it there the Holy Spirit will use it for furthering God's kingdom.

The Strange Activity of Preaching

In his book *Living Religions and a World Faith*, philosopher W. E. Hocking saw a characteristic of all living religions, which he describes as "the strange activity of preaching" ([New York: Macmillan, 1940], 37). Strangeness does not capture the monumental place preaching has in the Christian enterprise. "The strange activity of preaching" is at the heart of the Christian church. In fact, the Christian church is the result of preaching. There is "an indissoluble oneness of preaching and the Christian faith" (H. H. Farmer, *The Servant of the Word* [New York: Charles Scribners Sons, 1943], 7). You can't miss it, even reading the New Testament casually. From the first page, the Gospels record that John the Baptist came preaching, "Change your hearts and lives! Here comes the kingdom of heaven!" (Matt 3:2 CEB). He was proclaiming the inauguration of the kingdom and urging repentance so that the coming followers of Jesus (the church) would be ready for that kingdom. Jesus, too, came preaching. Matthew 4:17 says, "From that time Jesus began to announce, 'Change your hearts and lives! Here comes the kingdom of heaven!'" Mark 1:14-15 puts it this way: "After John was arrested, Jesus came into Galilee announcing God's good news, saying, 'Now is the time! Here comes God's kingdom! Change your hearts and lives, and trust this good news!'"

Who can read the New Testament and miss the significant passage where Jesus stood up in the synagogue and read from Isaiah, "The Spirit of the Lord is upon me, because the Lord has anointed me. He has sent me to preach good news to the poor, to proclaim release to the prisoners and recovery of sight to the blind, to liberate the oppressed, and to proclaim the year of the Lord's favor" (Luke 4:18-19 CEB)?

The church came to birth at Pentecost as Peter preached Jesus Christ, crucified and risen, the Savior of all humankind. It was at Pentecost that Christian preaching began. Yet, the theme of the preaching of Jesus and that of apostolic preaching is the same. Jesus came preaching God's kingdom, announcing that it is here, right now. After his crucifixion and resurrection, after the birth of the church at Pentecost, the apostles proclaimed that the kingdom had come. R. W. Dale said, "While Jesus came to preach the gospel, his chief objective in coming was that there might be a gospel to preach" (*The Atonement* [London: Congregational Union of England and Wales, 1905], 107).

The disciples in New Testament times preached. These apostles/leaders were itinerant evangelists who were primarily preachers. Their primary business was to proclaim the gospel. They knew themselves to be divinely commissioned to proclaim the gospel. Paul claims this calling with passion in Romans 10:14: "So how can they call on someone they don't have faith in? And how can they have faith in someone they haven't heard of? And how can they hear without a preacher?" The passion and conviction of Paul and the other apostles was so great that Paul would speak for them all, "If I preach the gospel, I have no reason to brag, since I'm obligated to do it. I'm in trouble if I don't preach the gospel" (1 Cor 9:16 CEB).

H. H. Farmer observed that preaching is not the only activity of the church—far from it—but without proclamation even compassionate acts to relieve human suffering can fall just short of the gospel, the changed hearts that sustain God's kingdom.

> Works of compassion, for example, such as must surely flow from any sharing in the mind and activity of Christ also find place in it. Yet preaching, in one form or another is obviously the basic, the pivotal thing, without which other activities have little power—(and only in an indirect and uncertain way do they) serve the saving, divine purpose which has entered history in Christ. It is not without significance that the gospel record of Christ's commission to his disciples put preaching first and then the healing of the sick. A work of

compassion even of the most devoted and sacrificial kind tells nothing per se about the gospel of the Kingdom of God. It only begins to speak of that when it is associated with, and interpreted by, the preaching of the gospel. (*The Servant of the Word*, 11–12)

So, "preaching is that divine, saving activity in history" (Farmer, *The Servant of the Word*, 15) that confronts us and brings the people together in relationships with God that sustain the church.

The Congregation's Experience with the Word of God

In the United States each weekend at least 300,000 sermons are preached, and since worship on Sunday morning is the primary experience with the word of God on the part of most Christians, it seems facetious to even ask a question about the importance of preaching. Yet that question gets raised with more frequency in the digital age because ordained ministers are no longer the only or most frequently consulted source of information about God or other spiritual matters. Even before the internet we went through long periods when preaching did not receive the attention it deserves. Enthused programmers in the church have told us at times that preaching was irrelevant. They behaved as if some other form of ministry should occupy center stage in the church and would be more effective than preaching in accomplishing what the church is about. During the ascent of the Sunday school movement in the twentieth century, it was Christian education; then it was therapeutic pastoral counseling after World War II; then it was missional social action; and then it was small groups. Each of these priorities was suggested by advocates as more important or more effective than preaching.

However, the lay Christian leaders have not become disinterested by competing priorities. Ask the people what they see as the primary task of their minister. Or better, let the district superintendent or bishop ask church leaders what they want in a pastor/leader. The most popular response will be: "We want a person who can preach and who cares about people." Church participants want a leader who will speak to the people for God and who will speak to God for the people.

Like me, readers who are ordained probably had a word like this spoken in their ordination service: "Take thou the authority to preach the word of God." This is not a disconnected word. In liturgical definitions, the true church is found "where the word of God is truly preached and the sacraments administered."

It is difficult to imagine the continuation of the church or the Christian faith without preaching. We have witnessed in recent years the faith staying alive in China in an underground or house-church mode, but when that story is told completely I think we will learn the story of the faithfulness of preaching. During a visit to China in 1979, I saw the bamboo curtain drawn back a bit. We couldn't meet publicly with Christians; we had to meet in secret. I remember being with three couples in a hotel room in Beijing. It was as near to what I imagine must have been in the early church when Christians gathered in the catacombs to worship.

We talked quietly, but we took the risk of quietly singing together old familiar gospel hymns like "Amazing Grace" and "What a Friend We Have in Jesus." They had memorized the words. I wondered how their practices differed in the underground church than when they could be together publicly in worship. So I asked, "What do you miss most?" Without hesitation they responded, "We miss most gathering publicly to worship with the community of faith and hearing the word of God proclaimed." They missed preaching.

That is the reason the government outlawed preaching—because the gospel proclaimed generates the church. That is the reason there could be no public proclamation of the word outside the few church buildings that were allowed to be open. This also happened in the Soviet Union and the Eastern Bloc behind the iron curtain. Preaching and witnessing outside the church were outlawed. Even those who are not part of the faith know the power of preaching.

Preaching and the Preacher

At its best, when it is most authentic, preaching and the preacher are intimately connected. Unless the message has gripped the messenger, the chances are it will not get the kind of hearing that will make a difference. Consider Phillip Brook's classic definition of preaching as "truth through personality": "Preaching is not simply the transference of theological ideas from one mind to another. The gospel message is being revealed through a person, whose own response to it will be a tremendous factor in its transmission" (Ronald E. Sleeth, *Proclaiming the Word* [Nashville: Abingdon, 1964], 27).

For the preacher to be believed when speaking to the people for God about what is true, she must be qualified by discipline and example:

> The way to understand and communicate the Christian faith is through disciplined participation in that faith. This is not an option for the preacher. How does one become qualified to talk of forgiveness, of penitence, of the death of Christ . . . read a good book on the subject? It is by obedience and sacrifice. Appropriation of the gospel is the minimum condition for approaching pulpit or podium. From the standpoint of the hearers, the qualities of the teller affect the response to the story. The decision that a message is worth listening to is the decision that the teller is worth listening to. If the speaker is not in her preaching, if her absence is evidenced by an overuse of clichés, quotations, and secondary sources, the hearers feel deceived and deprived. (Gerald Kennedy, *His Word through Preaching* [New York: Harper & Brothers, 1947])

We need to pray continually that when we preach we can speak God's words to the people with integrity and humility: "We don't preach about ourselves. Instead, we preach about Jesus Christ as Lord, and we describe ourselves as your slaves for Jesus' sake" (2 Cor 4:5 CEB). This will be possible only through consistent spiritual disciplines described in chapter 4. Effective Christian leadership, and preaching in particular, is dependent upon recognizing and acting on the fact that Christ lives in us. This is a direct result of our recognizing, claiming, and cultivating the presence of the indwelling Christ. Only the things that have happened to us can happen through us.

Confessional Preaching and Personal Limitations

Henri Nouwen told an old legend from the Talmud, which gives a graphic picture of the image of the gospel through us.

> Rabbi Yoshua Ben Levi came upon Elijah, the prophet, and asked him, "When will the Messiah come?"
> Elijah replied, "Go and ask him yourself."
> "Where is He?" asked the Rabbi.
> "Sitting at the Gates of the City."
> "But how shall I know him?"
> "He is sitting around the poor, covered with his wounds. The others unbind all their wounds at the same time and then bind them up again, but He unbinds only one at a time and binds it up again, saying to himself, 'Perhaps I shall be needed. If so, I must always be ready, so as not to delay for a moment.'" (Nouwen, *The Wounded Healer in Contemporary Society* [New York: Doubleday, 1979], 81)

This Talmud story suggests an important dimension of spiritual leadership—but more than that, the secret to Christian living—to attend to our woundedness, and be a healing presence for the woundedness of others.

The dynamic that facilitates that process best for the preacher is confessional preaching. In our preaching we must willingly open our lives to others, to be transparent as a visible reminder of what the gospel is all about.

William Barclay told the story about a court artist painting the portrait of Oliver Cromwell. Cromwell was afflicted with warts on his face. Thinking to please him, the court painter omitted the warts in the painting. When Cromwell saw it, he said, "Take it away, and paint me warts and all!" Reflecting on that, Barclay reminds us that the book of Acts aimed to show us the disciples emerging with the early church, warts and all (Barclay, *The Acts of the Apostles, Daily Study Bible* [Louisville, KY: Westminster John Knox, 1955]). It was with ordinary people like ourselves that Jesus set out to change the world.

Integrity and Transparency

Two dynamics must work in tandem. One, the messenger must be gripped by the message to the degree that there is at least a hint of incarnation. At the same time, the preacher must be himself or herself in all the uniqueness with which God has gifted each of us.

In our discussion of discipline in chapter 4, we warned against pretension and imitation being enemies of vital spirituality. This warning is relevant as we talk about preaching and the preacher. The preacher must be herself in all the uniqueness with which God has gifted her. To project or to seek to fit into a standardized pattern of spirituality or preaching is to miss the meaning of God's gracious creativity that made each one of us a unique, unrepeatable miracle of God.

In *Souls on Fire*, Elie Wiesel tells story after story of the leaders of Hasidic Judaism. One of those was Rebbe Zusia, who was chronically burdened with countless miseries and ailments. Yet, he was known most for his contagious happiness.

> His capacity for happiness was equaled only by his humility. Once he was heard groaning: "I am unworthy of addressing my prayers to You; I am not even worthy of giving You my tears. Instead—listen—I shall whistle. That's all." Before he died, he said: "When I shall face the celestial tribunal, I shall not be asked why I was not Abraham, Jacob or Moses. I shall be asked—why I was not Zusia." (Wiesel, *Souls on Fire* [New York, Summit Books, 1972], 119–20)

We can learn from Zusia, who was a preacher and follower of the great founder of Hasidism, Baal Shem. Recognizing and cultivating awareness of and giving expression to the indwelling Christ, as the core of Christian spiritual formation, is not to make us carbon copies of some great preacher, but rather to call forth the rich diversity of gifts within us and to empower us to express those gifts.

The dynamic that enables us to balance exercising our uniqueness and seeking to model Christlikeness is ongoing cultivation of the presence of the indwelling Christ.

In *The Living Reminder: Service and Prayer in Memory of Jesus Christ* (1981), Henri Nouwen describes ministers as a healing reminder, a sustaining reminder, and a guiding reminder. That cultivation of memory is exactly what preaching performs for the church: healing, sustaining, guiding. When Nouwen finished writing the book, he realized that he had discussed the minister as pastor, priest, and prophet. As pastors, we heal the wounds of the past. As priests, we sustain life in the present. As prophets, we guide others to the future.

Nouwen brought the biblical roles of ministry into conversation with pastoral psychology, and he united these three "memory" roles with prayer and service. Cultivating awareness of the indwelling Christ is keeping memory active. To the degree of this living awareness of the indwelling Christ the messenger and message will be linked, and incarnation will take place. The Word was made flesh then; the Word is to be made flesh now. The minister becomes the living reminder of Christ every day, and his message on Sunday is living witness to the living Christ.

Bishop William A. Quayle addressed the authentic witness connected to the people's lives through keen observation that allows preaching to name what is real:

> When this preacher comes to a Sunday in his journey through the week, people ask him, "Preacher man, where were you and what saw you while the work days were sweating at their toil?"
>
> And then of this preacher, we may say reverently, "He opened his mouth and taught them, saying, 'And there will be another though lesser Sermon on the Mount.'" And the auditors sit and shout under their breath, and say with their helped hearts, "Preacher, saw you and heard you that? You were well employed. Go out and listen and look another week and be very sure to come back and tell us what you heard and saw." (Quayle, *The Pastor-Preacher* [Cincinnati: Jennings & Graham, 1910], 310)

How can you through preaching be the visible, reliable reminder of Jesus to heal, sustain, and guide your congregation? We need to reflect on how our life preaches when it is out and about.

Chapter 7

Out and About

Somewhere along the way, I watched a TV program about the release of a number of wild turkeys into the wilderness of the southwestern United States, where naturalists were seeking to reestablish a strain of turkeys. A little radio transmitter was affixed to the back of each turkey, in order to track them and understand how they were doing. Imagine sitting at a screen and following the whereabouts of all those turkeys.

My imagination began to wonder what it would be like to have a tracking device affixed to my back (some of you are thinking about the smartphone in your pocket), so that my family, my best friends, and my church could follow my every move. Wow! Everyday? How would I like that?

As that thought occurs to me from time to time, I'm thinking about our lives as Christian leaders. Most Christian leaders have a smartphone with GPS (some including an application to "find my friends"), but leaders try to protect privacy and establish boundaries. Nevertheless our coming and going as leaders is being closely observed. What we do when we are out and about in our communities, how and with whom we spend our time is not only noted by those around us, it is crucial for self-examination. In fact, where and with whom we spend time may mean as much as our sermon.

During the Reformation, *coram Deo*, "in the presence of God" or "before the eyes of God," became the motivating spirit of the reformers. Nothing marked them more than an awe of the holy, majestic God who called men and women into relationship. As for them, so with us. We need to live, awed by the fact that all of private and public life is *coram Deo*, "in the presence of God," which means we must claim and stay aware of our identity as pastor-preacher-leader. We are not just leaders, we are spiritual leaders. In speaking for God, we have the responsibility of influencing God's people in God's direction. Within and outside the congregations we lead we are to be witnesses of the wholeness and holiness to which we are calling other people.

Most leaders struggle with what this means. It relates to the problem encountered by all Christ followers: how to be "in the world but not of the world." Spiritual leaders today navigate in a culture far more secular than Christian. Ironically, sometimes we have our toughest time navigating among those we seek to lead who have the distorted notion that "Christianity is about things of the spirit, not about things of the world." Recall Father Malloy from chapter 1:

> You were so human, Father Malloy,
>   taking a friendly glass sometimes with us,
>   siding with us who would rescue Spoon River

from the coldness and the dreariness of village morality.
....
You did not seem to be ashamed of the flesh;
you faced life as it is,
and as it changes.

How we move "out and about" in our places of leadership is critical and demands attention.

Pay Attention

We must keep our eyes open as we are out and about every day. When we look, we need to be sure we see. J. Oswald Sanders, in his classic book *Spiritual Leadership*, put it cryptically: "Eyes that look are common; eyes that see are rare" ([Chicago: Moody, 1994], 56). He was talking about leaders having the capacity to see what others miss, and also to see further than the immediate and the present. He was also talking about focus and attention.

To a marked degree, to what we pay attention determines who we are. Who we keep company with is the primary nutrient for our spiritual growth. In typical poignant style, a proverb expresses how important attention is: "Ears to hear and eyes to see—the Lord made them both" (Prov 20:12 CEB). Seeing and hearing are the primary dynamics when paying attention.

As leaders, we pay attention to life around us. This is essential especially for effective pastoral leadership. We need to know what's going on in the community; what are the civic/political issues. Who are the elected leaders? Who are the people who, though not elected or stated officials, are exerting influence? Naturally, this varies from place to place and the size of community and/or city.

This engagement may mean we volunteer to serve in community causes beyond our congregations (e.g., 56 percent of the Christian leaders who visit ministrymatters.com volunteer for an entity outside their church). For instance, nothing is more important to the population of any town or city than education. Also, I doubt if any local issue is in and out of the news more than public education. If we have "hearing ears and seeing eyes" and spend the time necessary to at least know the issues, and be able to converse sensibly, we may be able to exert leadership in this critical area of concern.

As we are out and about, we need to especially pay attention to those persons we relate to—perhaps more important, to those persons we have opportunity to relate to but don't.

A clergy friend, Buzz Stevens, shared about a nurse in training who went to a class one day where the professor announced there would be a pop quiz. She breezed through the questions until she came to the last one, "What is the first name of the woman who cleans this building?"

She thought it must be some kind of a joke. Whoever heard of that kind of a question on a test? She had seen the cleaning woman. She could describe her physically, but why should she know her name?

She handed in her test, leaving the last question unanswered. She asked the professor, "Are you going to count that last question on the final score?" "Absolutely," said the professor, "In your career you are going to meet many people. Each one is significant. Each person deserves your attention and care, even if all you do is smile and say hello."

In addition to our sermons, our pastoral counseling, and our formal teaching settings, we should communicate that we are concerned about life. And as shepherds, leaders are concerned for all the sheep. So we are called to develop relationships with those who are a part of our "flock" but also those who are "outside the fold."

Who We Spend Time With

Those we lead notice who we spend time with. A common complaint about pastors is "playing favorites." We run the risk of such an accusation if we don't ask ourselves, Am I investing my time with the right people? This means not only ministering to those who need us but spending time with those we need.

When I first entered the ministry, there was discussion about whether a pastor should have close friends in the congregation. Early on, the usual admonition from my elders was, "Don't get too close to any of your people, even your leaders. Your friends should be outside the congregation." Similar advice is sometimes given to business leaders, who can be required to end someone's employment. That advice, which is based in hierarchy, continues to confuse me; taken seriously, it is a hard road to walk. Added to the primary admonition is the broad advice, "Keep your distance."

Two principles have served me well. One, I need friends, and where I find them is not the issue. Two, I attend to boundaries. I don't share with all my friends the same kind of relationship or the same content from my life journey. I may share with friends outside the church struggles related specifically to the congregation or about an issue I may be having with a church member. I would not share that same conversation with a person inside the church where I serve.

The truth is, most leaders do not have a lot of friends. The very nature of friendship demands time and the kind of emotional involvement that allows for a few deep friendships. Friends on Facebook are not deep, but how we share ourselves generally with followers is a critical issue.

The Gospel through Our Person

E. Stanley Jones, the renowned missionary evangelist who worked primarily in India, was acutely aware of a practice that continues to challenge us today: our public witness is intimately connected to our ability to witness publicly. He insisted that our words must ring true to our life, and our life must reinforce our words. Our witness in the public arena, our way of being in the world, must align with the content of the public expression of our faith.

Gandhi drove this point home to E. Stanley Jones. After sharing his desire that Christianity no longer be identified as foreign but become a natural part of the spiritual landscape of India, Jones asked Gandhi what he must do to make that possible. Gandhi replied:

> I would suggest, first, that all of you Christians, missionaries and all, must begin to live more like Jesus Christ.... Second, I would suggest that you must practice your religion without adulterating or toning it down.... Third, I would suggest that you must put your emphasis on love, for love is the center and soul of Christianity.... Fourth, I would suggest you study the non-Christian religions and cultures more sympathetically in order to find the good that is in them, so that you might have more sympathetic approach to the people. (E. Stanley Jones, *Christ of the Indian Road* [Nashville: Abingdon, 1925], 118–19)

This advice is as valid for us now as it was then in India.

Paul makes it clear that the gospel is communicated through our person. In Galatians 4, he makes the case. He pulls back the curtain of his own inner soul, revealing his anguish and pain, his personal limitations, his feelings of failure, his overwhelming sense of appreciation. You feel the deep emotion and tenderness in his word, "You didn't look down on me or reject me, but you welcomed me as if I were an angel from God, or as if I were Christ Jesus!" (Gal 4:14 CEB).

As should be the case with all Christian leaders, Paul's overarching commitment is to those he considered his spiritual children. He is pulling out all the stops at the emotional center of his whole being as he appeals for a response to himself as a person. He talks about those who "preach Christ because of their selfish ambition. They are insincere, hoping to cause me more pain while I'm in prison" (Phil 1:17 CEB). He responds to these circumstances:

> What do I think about this? Just this: since Christ is proclaimed in every possible way, whether from dishonest or

> true motives, I'm glad and I'll continue to be glad. I'm glad because I know that this will result in my release through your prayers and the help of the Spirit of Jesus Christ. It is my expectation and hope that I won't be put to shame in anything. Rather, I hope with daring courage that Christ's greatness will be seen in my body, now as always, whether I live or die. (Phil 1:18-20 CEB)

The New English Bible (v. 20) emphasizes the person's witness, because Paul speaks "so boldly that now as always the greatness of Christ will shine out clearly in my *person*, whether through life or through death."

In chapter 6 on preaching and the preacher, I asserted that in our preaching there should be at least a hint of the incarnation (God with us) when we speak to the people for God. For the Christian leader, who we are as we are out and about is as critical as who we are in the pulpit or when speaking for God.

An example of embodying the Spirit was seen in Mother Teresa, the saint who gave her life for the poorest of the poor. She observed in her book, *A Gift for God*:

> We all long for heaven where God is, but we have it in our power to be in heaven with Him right now—to be happy with Him at this very moment. But being happy with Him now means:
>   loving as He loves,
>   helping as He helps,
>   giving as He gives,
>   serving as He serves,
>   rescuing as He rescues,
>   being with Him for all the twenty-four hours, and

> touching Him in His distressing disguise.
> (New York: HarperCollins, 1996)

In his humanity, Jesus was the incarnation of God, God's human representation of himself. As God sent someone in fully human form to represent (re-present) him, so Jesus calls re-presenters, and we accept that purpose. We are that in our preaching and teaching, in our leadership within the congregation, and we are also that in our out-and-about presence in the community.

The gospel must be seen in the person who seeks to communicate it. As another who spoke for God, Paul made a bold plea: "I beg you to be like me, brothers and sisters" (Gal 4:12 CEB). It could be seen as arrogance except Paul had been willing to reveal his full humanity. He had a serious physical infirmity. While we do not know what the affliction was, we know that it was chronic, very painful, humiliating, and repulsive.

Paul rejoiced that the Galatians did not "despise" or "reject" him (see Gal 4:12 KJV). One meaning for this kind of contempt (*exoutheneo* in Greek) might be "spit out." The Galatians did not spit in Paul's presence as people were accustomed to doing when they wanted to ward off an evil spirit. This kind of language indicates the extremity of Paul's affliction, which apparently seemed repulsive. "Though my poor health burdened you, you didn't look down on me or reject me" (Gal 4:14 CEB).

Yet Paul still appeals through himself: "be like me." It is Paul's ultimate appeal with the Galatians: "I beg you to be like me, brothers and sisters, because I have become like you! You haven't wronged me" (Gal 4:12 CEB). This is the gospel's appeal. As Christian leaders we are to be the visible gospel.

Recognize Your Strength

The word of the gospel is always a personal word. We do not know what Paul's affliction was, whether malaria, epilepsy, eye trouble, migraine, or some other malady. In those days sickness was regarded as God's punishment for sins, so it would have been natural for the Galatians to treat Paul as if he were a devil, not a messenger from God. Paul apparently handled his affliction in such a Christlike manner that even his limitation became an asset. What we do with our limitations is not only a measure of our faith but determines the effectiveness of our ministry and witness.

Limitations do not have to limit.

Thomas Fuller provides balance for the tension points of life: "Let not thy will roar, when thy power can but whisper" (Earnie Larsen and Carol Hegarty, *Believing in Myself* [Upper Saddle River, NJ: Prentice-Hall, 1991]). We sometimes go to extremes in responding to life and seeking to be an effective spiritual leader. One extreme is to adopt a victim mentality; the other is a pretension to strength and sufficiency.

Gary Larson, now retired, made a powerful social witness through his *Far Side* cartoons. In one cartoon he pictured a woman sitting on an overstuffed sofa, her hair in curlers and in her right hand she is holding a broom. She has either been at work or she is going to work. In the left hand she holds the phone. You look on the scene and see her there in that overstuffed sofa surrounded by large fish bowls filled with all sorts of swimming creatures. She says, "Well, that is the way it happens, Sylvia. I kissed this frog, he turned into a prince, we got married and wham—I am stuck at home with a bunch of Pollywogs."

That's the victim mentality. It is easy for us to fall into that snare. Preachers and people who have a special calling and are involved in "full-time Christian service" often do this. I believe it is a perversion of humility. We develop a persecution complex. We take ourselves too seriously. We think the kingdom enterprise is really hanging on our activity. We don't know how to fail gracefully. If things don't go our way, we think it is because we are not being faithful. We play the martyr role. If we don't say it, we act it out: poor me! It is a role we play in a drama that we keep writing as we go along. We cast ourselves as losers and in scene after scene, act after act.

Closely akin to casting ourselves as losers is the practice somewhat less extreme but still a dimension of the victim mentality: drowning ourselves in negative thoughts. When we think less of ourselves than we are, we think less of what God can do in and through us.

A balanced rhythm is this: We must not deny our weaknesses but honestly face and share them; yet we must not spend all our time trying to overcome them. We need to recognize our strengths as soon as possible, and try to improve them.

One of the prayers I utter regularly was sent to my wife, Jerry, by a Roman Catholic nun with whom she had spent two days in retreat. She had shared with Sister Mary her struggle with low self-esteem, so Sister Mary sent her this prayer, urging Jerry to pray daily, "O Lord, Help me to believe the truth about myself, no matter how beautiful it is." I borrowed that prayer from Jerry and I pray it often.

Support outside Formal Structures

We often find support outside formal structures. This support relates to how and with whom we spend our time. We tend to gravitate to people whom we like, who are usually people like us. We are comfortable with them because we share common interests. It is normal to want to spend time with them; yet the persons who can help us most may be people unlike us.

When I was young in the ministry and began to have leadership responsibilities, I recognized my limitations and acknowledged my inexperience. In rural Mississippi, we called it gumption. As a budding theologian, I soon began to call it grace. I had the gumption, or was given the grace, to willingly ask people for help. I soon discovered that help would best come from persons who were "successful" in their job or profession.

At different times along the way, it was a building contractor, a public school superintendent, a symphony conductor, the CEO of an international specialty chemical company, an investment manager. Along with individuals such as these, I also sought to relate to the persons in my community who were involved in faith-based ministries not intimately connected to a congregation. For the most part I simply sought to hear how these persons were doing their jobs. With some, according to how the relationship functioned and the level of my trust and respect, I would present problems or issues and seek advice.

In Memphis, while serving my last congregation for twelve years as senior minister, my two favorite clergy friends were Adrian Rogers and Doug Bailey. They were vastly different from each other and from me. Adrian was senior pastor of Bellevue Baptist Church, a national leader among conservative Southern Baptists. Doug was the rector of Calvary Episcopal Church, one of the most liberal churches in the city, and he was a part of the preaching conferences of the National Cathedral in Washington. I remember with joy sharing with Adrian in a group of a dozen men, six from each of our churches, studying together Stephen Covey's *7 Habits of Highly Effective People*. I also recall with gratitude preaching in Calvary's noon Lenten worship services and the long conversations on theology and the problems in our city that I had with Doug Bailey.

If we need it, want it, are honest in asking for it, and treat people well, when they respond, we will get the support we need.

Available in Love

When we are out and about, we need to be available in love. As we move about in our community, pay attention, listen, become involved in issues that have impact upon the community, care and serve in an at-large kind of way, a kind of congregation "not our own" develops. The "fallout" of that ministry is often as significant and fulfilling as our "in church" ministry. More often than not, we are not the initiator but the responder.

Chapter 7

One of my fondest memories is of an "outside congregation" in San Clemente, California, where I planted and served a United Methodist church. Being a church planter may require more attention to the broader community than being the pastor of an established congregation. Even so, when you become a representative of Christ, the defining boundaries of who and where you serve is wider than your territory.

Leo Fessenden became a member of the California congregation. He owned and operated a music store. Scores of young people were in and out of his store daily. Though he would not have seen it this way, Leo became a sort of priest to these young people. I'm sure the young people didn't think of him in that light, but they went to him to share their problems and needs, their hopes and dreams, their failures and disappointments. During a five-year ministry in San Clemente, scores of young people, who had little or no contact with our church at all, came to see me because of Leo. In most cases, I discovered that Leo had already performed the most important ministry, and I simply added my supportive concern.

I remember a group of these young people coming to see me when they learned I was moving to another city. They were a motley crew. Many of the fellows had long hair and beards (that was before beards were popular); the girls were dressed in the rebellious garb of the day. On the street, they would have been stereotyped as "hippies," "dropouts," or "delinquents." They would have felt out of place in our congregation on Sunday morning, and many of my parishioners would have felt out of place with them. They were not the kind of youth that are usually in church on Sunday morning. Through misty eyes I looked at those young people and remembered a significant involvement with almost all of them. There was an unmarried young woman who had baby. There was a fellow who spent three months in juvenile hall. There was a second fellow who had been caught in the tentacles of drugs. All of them had experimented with marijuana, and many of them had tried LSD and different barbiturates. One had spent a week in our home as a runaway. One of them was, even then, paying me twenty-five dollars per month on a loan I had arranged for him, in order to pay the hospital bill of the young girl pregnant with his child (he repaid the entire amount). One of them had gone through a long period of depression because his mother had committed suicide.

My relationship with these young people had come primarily through Leo Fessenden in the music store. Because he was available to them, listened to them, cared about them, did for them what he could, they trusted me when I was recommended by him as a person with whom they could relate.

They gave me a going-away present that day, and I treasure it. But most of all I treasure a note that accompanied the gift. It read:

> We don't really know how to say it—but because "you cared" we are going to miss you. We never attended—much less belonged to your church—but we always felt you were one of us. You never had easy answers for us, but you were there when we needed help, and as you will remember the help we needed wasn't simple to give, but you gave it and we are grateful. As we say farewell, we hope that your God is standing outside your window smiling, because we know he

is as proud as we are of you. We wished that we could have made this presentation to you before your congregation, but we are sure you understand.

With all our love.

I have had leadership honors in my life, more than I deserve, but no honor has exceeded the gratitude those young people showed me. I miss the mark of the high calling of Christ much of the time in my life. I am rather tough on myself, and know that I often fall far short of the glory of God. So memories like this of these young people are important, reminding me that is the point at which God will ultimately judge me—whether I have been available in love, which is a way of asking whether, as I am out and about, am I being Christ to others?

Chapter 8

Taking Care of Ourselves in the Everyday

In the previous chapter, we focused on the importance of who we are and what we do as we move out and about in our ministry. We continue that discussion focusing on taking care of ourselves in the everyday.

The dropout rate among clergy is shocking. The last statistics I have seen indicate that 35–40 percent of women exit the ministry in their first appointment. The primary cause given is the rejection of the congregation of a woman as leader. I believe this is changing primarily for two reasons: more deliberate and sound biblical teaching, and the outstanding leadership women are providing when given the opportunity. More generally, 40 percent of all clergy leave the ministry during their first five years out of seminary or after ordination. The primary causes for this are moral failure and burnout; the two are connected. In my conversations with bishops, district superintendents, or judicatory leaders, having to relieve a pastor of his or her ministry because of moral failure is often sadly noted, while divorce among clergy is no longer a surprising issue.

It is true that who we keep company with is a primary nutrient for our spiritual growth and effectiveness in ministry. It is also true that the practical expression of our ministry has dimensions that thwart character development, our growth in holiness, and our spiritual sensitivity. These factors can become "demons" that work slyly to undermine not only our effectiveness but our very calling. If we are going to take care of ourselves as leaders, we must stay aware of these demonic forces. They have the potential of undercutting who we are and what God has called us to be and do.

Naming the Demons

Demonic is a strong word, used here to name systemic forces that undermine and harm the good that we would do. There are forces, and even practical expressions of ministry, that become barriers to growth and seeds for failure. These forces are not usually intrinsic to the location where we engage in ministry; rather the forces exert effects on our Christian character. I think these forces are expressions of original sin.

Taking care of ourselves involves doing battle with these demons. An obvious, but seldom acknowledged, force is what I call the "f-dimension"—fear of failure—and the source of this fear does have to do with our original sin. In fact, some would identify this fear as the primary expression of original sin: pride.

Pastors are not exempt. In your next meeting of pastors and ministry leaders, note the conversation. How many speak of the number of persons in worship the previous Sunday? The annual budget? The current membership number, and how many of those had become members under current leadership? The rumors about possible pastoral appointments? What does the conversation say about what we consider success in ministry?

None of us wants to fail, so a crippling fear of failure causes us to spend too much time and energy on an organizational agenda and on the church as an institution. As a result, we don't pay enough attention to our inner life, to our family wholeness, and to our own spirituality. In the process, we become generic leaders of an organization rather than really becoming faith-energized leaders whose style, values, relationships, and priorities identify us as distinctively Christian leaders.

Fear of failure drives us to the point that we fail to pay attention to what is lacking in our personal lives. To show how pernicious and destructive this is, consider the fact that we minimize personal disasters and family failures, such as divorce, and see these as more acceptable than failure in ministry.

It is an ominous reality: our fear of failure is a dominant dynamic in our lives. And when it becomes pronounced, as it so often does, we do not seek the personal spiritual renewal we need.

Closely akin to the fear of failure is a second issue, which is also an expression of pride: hunger for position, privilege, and power. Though a twin to our fear of failure, it is somewhat different. Our drive for achievement, for promotion and prestige, lead us to think we need to move to a bigger assignment, a larger congregation, and a higher salary. This preoccupation prevents us from paying attention to our present assignment and our own personal renewal. In an itinerant, episcopal appointment system, as we have in The United Methodist Church, we move regularly from one congregation to another. We know we are not going to stay in the church we now serve for the rest of our ministry. If we allow this fact to become a dominant force in how we orient our life, a destructive thing will happen. As we thirst for prestige, power, and position that would come if we moved to some more desirable or attractive assignment, almost unconsciously we begin thinking and even scheming of clever ways to make the move happen, so we spend our energy to that end.

If the move doesn't happen, two destructive results are likely. One, our fear of failure begins to rule more stringently, too often bringing depression. Two, we are likely to move into a pattern of overachievement. When we are not given the opportunity for promotion, many of us think we will not be recognized unless we achieve more in our present assignment. So we drive ourselves and others, sometimes mercilessly without any attempt to test our presuppositions, or keep an accurate perspective. This overachieving dynamic almost always takes a terrible toll on our spouses, children, church members, and ourselves.

Connected with both these "demons" is job security, which is the normal concern of all persons, especially for persons responsible for families. We pastors often joke about ordination meaning a "vow of poverty." But how we deal with job security and material support is no joking matter. There is good reason for some religious orders requiring the vow of poverty. Jesus knew that financial anxiety is an important matter, and he talked a lot about it.

Think about it this way. We envy people who are rich. When we hear of people inheriting fortunes, we say "lucky people." When we hear of women or men winning rich prizes through their own industry and skill, we're willing to admit that we would gladly be in their places. We imagine the sense of security and the relief from financial strain that wealth could bring, of the desirable things it could purchase, of the opportunity it would give for doing good, and after considering all this, we conclude that it is good to be rich.

Jesus taught otherwise. He even suggested we should be concerned about being rich. "His words startled the disciples, so Jesus told them again, 'Children, it's difficult to enter God's kingdom! It's easier for a camel to squeeze through the eye of a needle than for a rich person to enter God's kingdom'" (Mark 10:24-25 CEB).

These general observations about wealth make the case that it is exceedingly easy to misplace values. Each of us is accountable in our own hearts, within the context of a particular vocational setting and personal life situation. Some temptations are peculiar to the ministry and to our vocation—some of which I wrestle with almost daily—that would threaten to pervert ambition and center it not in God's kingdom but in ourselves. Personal security is one driver of selfishness, addiction, and weakness, so we need to pay attention.

Even before the quest for safety becomes rampant and wreaks havoc in our daily functioning, we should be regularly asking ourselves, Where do I place my security? Have I included God in my planning? If not, are there adjustments I need to make before my financial situation becomes crippling? Do I need more, or is it rather a matter of wanting more?

We can deal with the temptations and these demons that come with our vocation by continually asking questions like these:

- Am I resisting image-building by living as transparently as possible?
- Am I dealing with the conceit that comes from the applause of others?
- Am I keeping my calling clear, resisting both the temptation for security and competitive spirit?
- Am I defensive when asked about the use of my time and the consistency of my spiritual disciplines?

I've been talking about claiming and preserving our identity as pastors, making the foundational assertion that all the permanent fruit of our ministry is dependent upon the content of our character. I rehearsed the demonic forces of pride, dimensions of our professional ministry that thwart character development and our growth in holiness and spiritual sensitivity, undermining not only our effectiveness but our very calling as spiritual leaders.

Where you point your attention, to a marked degree, determines who you are. This is the primary way we take care of ourselves: keeping company with those who can nurture us and hold us accountable. We have two ways of staying focused and accountable.

The Discipline of Christian Conferencing

The classic spiritual disciplines are essential for our spiritual growth: prayer, scripture reading, fasting, Holy Communion, confession, solitude, submission, service, and generosity. In the Methodist/Wesleyan tradition, which considers these disciplines "the means of grace," we include Christian conferencing.

Most leaders have practiced conferencing to some degree, but some have not overtly practiced it as a spiritual discipline. Conferencing is deliberate and intentional Christian conversation.

This discipline came alive for me through E. Stanley Jones and the Christian Ashram Movement. Jones was a world-renowned missionary/evangelist, with most of his work in India. He was a pioneer in cross-cultural mission and interfaith dialogue. He witnessed effectively to the intellectual community.

Hindu holy men had their "ashrams," places where they lived and taught. Persons spend weeks, some of them months, in these ashrams "at the feet" of these holy men. Jones was impressed by that dynamic, so he established "the Christian Ashram," basically a one-week experience, in a place where persons lived together to study, pray, work, and share. But in the Christian Ashram, there were no "holy men," no guru through which the teaching and sharing evolved. There were no titles; all were "brother" or "sister."

Two principles were operative in the Ashram experience: everybody is a teacher, everybody is being taught. Brother Stanley believed that whenever Christians come together in Jesus's name, the resources are there for edification and response to need. It was a community of "Christian conferencing." You may have known this discipline through some form of an accountability group. The Methodist movement began in societies and bands with the same accountability practices.

The fruit of Christian conferencing is rich. We experience three primary results:

- We receive encouragement and challenge.
- If we are faithful together in covenant, we keep one another honest and hold one another accountable.
- The relationships become a source of guidance, particularly the testing of guidance.

We recognize and affirm that divine guidance comes primarily from scripture and the living Christ, through the Holy Spirit and in prayer conversation. Yet other persons in a shared Christian life together are also channels for guidance. As we remain centered in Christ and come alive to his indwelling presence, we can be Christ to, and receive Christ from, the persons we meet.

When I am leading a retreat, I often begin by inviting persons to share a love greeting. I ask them to select someone they may know only casually, or not at all, get the person's first name, and exchange a greeting in this fashion: in pairs, facing each other, holding hands, one will say, "Mary, the love of Jesus in me greets the love of Jesus in you, and brings us together in the name of the Father, the Son, and the Holy Spirit." Then the other person shares the same greeting. I instruct them ahead of time to sit quietly after each has shared the greeting without any comment, reflecting on what they are feeling.

It is amazing how the mood in the entire gathering changes; the depth of holy silence is palpable. It is not unusual to see people wiping tears, and persons witnessing to a vivid awareness of the presence of Christ. To be sure, this is in a special setting, but it suggests an ever-present possibility. The more we cultivate our awareness of the indwelling Christ, the more we resonate to his aliveness in others and discern his guidance through them.

When Jesus said, "You are the light of the world," he affirmed this principle of guidance. We know ourselves as "light," by which others walk and are guided. How absolutely crucial it is to have a few people upon whom we depend as light. We might call these persons our "watch-out friends." They watch out for us. We invite them to do this, and it is a mutual relationship. The foundational dynamic of the relationship is twofold. First, we respect one another. Having the esteem of others is fundamental to our personal well-being. When personal regard is mutually expressed, the second dynamic is possible: we can share freely and openly.

These watch-out friends are essential and probably the persons we covenant with for Christian conferencing. They will test our honesty. Scripture instructs us to get rid of all deceit and hypocrisy (1 Pet 2:1). Character counts; leadership is dependent upon it. Honesty is the bedrock of character. Christian leaders need persons with whom honest criticism is welcomed. Proverbs 27:5 says, "A public correction is better than hidden love." It is more loving to confront others about a particular fault or bothersome issue than to allow them to continue as they are. In Christian conferencing, we show that we really care through constructive criticism, and we become better persons and certainly better leaders.

We can trust our watch-out friends to question our clarity. Nothing is more essential for good communication than clarity. Because we think we are clear in our convictions and what we seek to communicate, that isn't always the case. Our convictions, even our beliefs, often need to be tested for clarity.

Our watch-out friends also observe and check our passion. I doubt if anyone can be a good and effective leader without passion, but the way passion is received and modulated is a huge dimension in how effective we are. We need persons we trust to check our passion, to slow us down or speed us up.

God doesn't hold us responsible for results, but God does hold us responsible for what we do and how we do it. As leaders, we need trusted friends to help us determine how we do what we believe God is calling us to do. We also need trusted friends to test what we perceive as God's guidance.

CHAPTER 9

Little Foxes That Spoil the Vines

The Song of Songs, as it is known by its title in Hebrew, is attributed by ancient scribes to Solomon, who was born to Bathsheba. After Solomon assumed the throne, he had seven hundred royal wives and three hundred secondary wives (or concubines; 1 Kings 11:3). The Song of Songs is a collection of love poems between a man and a woman, celebrating their relationship as lovers. As with the book of Esther, God is not mentioned in the Song of Songs.

In the book of Genesis, God establishes a partnership between the first man and first woman, and affirms the physical union of husband and wife (Gen 2:18-25). This union becomes known as the appropriate expression of human sexuality in marriage after Israel's exile from the promised land and in early Christian understandings.

In Song 4, the man refers to his lover as "my sister, my bride." In Song 2, the woman describes her lover with multiple images. In 2:14 she extols his attractive features: "Let me catch sight of you; let me hear your voice! The sound of your voice is sweet, and the sight of you is lovely" (CEB).

Then in Song 2:15 comes a strange interruption and puzzling word: "Catch foxes for us—those little foxes that spoil vineyards, now that our vineyards are in bloom!" (CEB). In this beautiful poem, the foxes are symbolic. If the blossoming vineyard is taken to mean the romance between the couple, then the foxes represent potential problems that could damage their relationship. The woman is paying attention to the relationship and is beseeching her lover to protect their love from anything that could harm it. The beloved wants her lover to address and remove dangers, obstacles, and threats to their love. As they pay attention to the "little things," the lovers will continue to pursue sexual intimacy.

The "little" foxes seem to be the little things, the things overlooked, that often spoil things of value. This is certainly true in leadership and our practice of ministry. An often-quoted proverb says, "Men trip not on mountains; they stumble on stones."

Relevant but Grounded

As observed in chapter 5, it's not enough to know theology and scripture, not enough to know good leadership principles and get along well with people. If we are to be faithful shepherds of our people, if we fulfill our calling to be prophets and pastors with integrity, we need to know the unique needs, longing, hurts, and aspirations of the people within our reach. We need to discern and examine the social sources of the pain and suffering, such as addictions, economic structures, and failing political or educational systems. Do we know the questions that people are asking? We need to at least be "on speaking terms" with culture, and there is more than one culture in your neighborhood. We need to be relevant.

Relevance to the people who need the gospel is critical, but relevance can become a little fox that destroys the vines. The call to relevance seems to get more urgent every week as the culture becomes more complicated. This is one of the stones we are apt to stumble over. We can be so focused on the cultural change that we hold theology too loosely. We can so identify with the people around us that we forget we are ambassadors of Christ's kingdom. We can be so focused on "making worship relevant" that the medium becomes the message. When we try to be too relevant, we not only fail in our mission as Christ's followers but we fail the people we are called to serve. Following Jesus answers the deepest human needs, and yet many of those needs are the consequence of change.

Change

Seeking to be relevant often means adapting to change. It's sometimes said that in the church the only one who likes change is the wet baby in the nursery. But change happens, and most of us are quite resistant to change. Many of us fear change.

Some change has been exhilarating: the mapping of the human genome system, and the wiring of our world with the internet. Our heads swim at the thought of these changes. But some changes have been unnerving: the horrifying scourge of terrorism, the rapid development of computers that may soon surpass human intelligence, the stunning growth of human knowledge. At present, human knowledge doubles every two years, but it is estimated that knowledge will double every seventy-three days by the year 2020. We are baffled and wonder, how are we going to keep up?

The Christian leader must learn to adapt. We must also constantly assess our perspective and our way of "doing things." Sameness and routine often result in inertia. Change may be the needed dynamic to move us out of what become our ruts of mediocrity and boredom.

Some changes are thrust upon us, such as a health crisis or involuntarily having to change leadership positions. Then there are the changes we deliberately choose. In either case, the best way to prepare for the inevitable is to learn how to be adaptable. The way we learn to be adaptable is to move out of our comfort zone occasionally and try something new. In such moves, we gain confidence; we push back our self-perceived limits and grow in our ability to cope.

Changes for Christian leaders include worship style—from traditional to contemporary—or music, the times of worship, adoption of a new management structure, the forging of a new direction in ministry and mission, or moving from focusing "inside" to moving "outside" the walls.

Dealing with change within our congregation, or in the faith community we lead, whether imposed or chosen, is where the "little foxes" do their destructive work.

Dealing with the disharmony and disruption is the kind of change that requires careful attention to how we talk and how we listen. It's a big mistake to think that talking is more important than listening. Relationship is far more important than explanation. Nothing affirms a person more than being listened to. We learn by listening, but we also establish trust. So in the midst of change we need to listen enough to make our words and explanations count.

When we need to speak, speak clearly and honestly, as transparently as possible. It is pernicious, in the midst of controversy and change, to try to hide something. Even a hint of deception can be deadly. If we have listened, and if we speak respectfully with and to those who disagree with what we are doing, then we can move forward with energy and without apology.

Dealing with Difficult People

Difficult people are a presence to be reckoned with in far more places than when we are dealing with change, and in far more relationships than within our congregation or ministry community. They are in our family network, civic groups, community organizations, and our social networks. They are the gossips, the bullies, the manipulators, the intimidators, the blamers, the criticizers, the complainers, the whiners—just fill in the blank. The "little foxes" can use these people readily to "destroy the vines."

We are never more like Jesus than when we love the unlovely.

First Peter is sent to Christian communities spread throughout Asia Minor. These Christians are called "God's chosen strangers in the world" (1 Pet 1:1 CEB). The writer knew these strangers were being harassed and that harassment could cause growth or bitterness. Character—how they acted and how they lived together—would be their primary witness. He urged them to be holy: "But, as obedient children, you must be holy in every aspect of your lives" (1 Pet 1:14-15 CEB). He concluded a section of his teaching with this admonition: "Finally, all of you be of one mind, sympathetic, lovers of your fellow believers, compassionate, and modest in your opinion of yourselves. Don't pay back evil for evil or insult for insult. Instead, give blessing in return. You were called to do this so that you might inherit a blessing" (1 Pet 3:8-9 CEB). This is the way Christians are to live together, so certainly there is some guidance here for dealing with difficult people. To be sure, as we are urged to pray for one another, that injunction has heavy implications for our relation to difficult people, and especially within a congregation or ministry community. We are to pray persistently.

We are to respond respectfully to one another. Christian leaders must take the lead in being compassionate and humble, not repaying "evil for evil or insult for insult." What a difficult word to accept and act on! We deal with difficult people by blessing them; in fact, it is in blessing difficult people that we are blessed.

The word *bless* in scripture means to make happy, to bring comfort and joy, or to praise. Doesn't complimenting courageously convey blessing in various circumstances? If we value persons, believing that even difficult individuals are of sacred worth, we can honestly compliment. We can compliment readily if we remember that nothing affirms a person more than being listened to. So we need to listen enough to establish trust and make our words and explanations count.

Power

Leaders have power, and power can be seductive. Some observers compare leadership with seduction, even suggesting that individuals with an interest in leadership are seduced by the power relationship. I'm sure this often happens, so I'm sounding a warning that the power we seek in our leadership roles can be seductive, blinding us to our weakness and frailty as ordinary human beings. The cure for this blindness is to stay aware of the fact that the power that comes with our leadership vocation can give us not only a false sense of security but a distorted notion of capability.

A false sense of security is destructive. Many leaders who fail in ministry, both in terms of moral or ethical failure and failure in being fulfilled by their achievement, do so because of a false sense of security. This is the reason we need to practice the discipline of Christian conferencing and be in intentional relationship with "watch-out friends" who hold us accountable. Just as leaders have a marked responsibility for the action of the people they lead, we need trusted persons to hold us accountable for our actions.

Chapter 9

Money

In the previous chapter, we briefly discussed money in the context of security. We need to reflect more about it, because money is a bane and a blessing. Few things get leaders into more trouble. It is a blessing without which we can't fulfill much of the ministry and mission to which we are called. It is a bane, used by the "little foxes" to destroy the fruit of the ministry, when the leader is not a good steward.

Those we lead take notice and are usually very aware about how we use and manage money, both personally and in our professional life. Our ability to teach and encourage good stewardship depends on how we personally handle money.

There are three failures or characteristics that may call our leadership into question.

- *Failure to pay our debts.* Some folks take great delight in discovering and sharing the failures of their own leaders. So don't ever assume this failure will not eventually be known. This is an issue almost from the beginning of our ministry. Education required for ministry often puts persons in debt before they begin. This makes it even more critical to live according to our means, not spending more than we earn and making our debt even greater.

- *Stinginess.* It is interesting that people want us to be conservative in handling the financial resources of the congregation or our ministry organization, but to appear to be stingy as a person has negative impacts on followers. No one wants to follow a "Scrooge." This is not solely a financial matter.

Stinginess affects the whole life in terms of whether we are unwilling to give and share. There is nothing stingy about the gospel, and no way to connect grace and stinginess. Leaders must be generous people.

- *Always having your hand out.* That's the idiom laypeople use when they talk about their leader expecting special favors, "he always has his hand out." There is a vast difference between being a gracious recipient of the generosity people want to extend and always expecting them to be generous to us personally.

Don't be intimidated by money, and don't show special favor to those who have money. Don't allow them to use their money to leverage their agenda. If we are wise, we will not put the more wealthy persons in our congregations in a special category as we look for leadership. But alas, inadvertently perhaps, we will not consider them as needy spiritually as anyone else.

In the next chapter we will consider the invasion of "little foxes that spoil the vineyards" in relation to time and family. Here I make an important observation about money and family. Don't act poor! It is important in relation to family, especially children, that we not associate our financial limitations with the church. Young children can't process claims that being a preacher means economic sacrifice. Don't communicate to your children that the church is not paying you enough for a vacation to Disneyland. Connecting the lack of money with the church gives children a distorted picture of the church, and not a positive one. Children need to be reminded of how wonderful it is that their father or mother has a job that allows tremendous freedom; unlike attorneys, doctors, office workers, most teachers, and most other jobs, a pastor or ministry leader has the freedom to be present for an afternoon concert, soccer practice, or other special school events. So save for the vacation, a vacation you can afford, and take advantage of the "perks" of the lifestyle your vocation provides, thus making your children's understanding of your job positive.

Criticism

An old saying was right, "Criticism is something you can avoid easily—by saying nothing, doing nothing, and being nothing." For the leader, criticism is inevitable. How we handle it determines whether it becomes a "little fox that spoils the vines."

John Wesley talked about pride in terms of not seeing someone we seriously disagree with as having something to teach us. Perhaps more than any others, those persons may teach us that we don't know what we don't know.

Many leaders respond to criticism by not responding; they disregard it. There may be occasions when that is the right response, but we need to be sure. We must be careful that we don't allow our pride to diminish the value of others' assessment of us. If the criticism is of a nature that we know most people will disregard, then we can do the same. But be careful; it's true, many people will believe anything. It is also true that many people especially relish seeing fault in people who are thought to have no fault. Note how the news media responds to public leaders, especially religious leaders, who have moral failures.

However we choose to handle it, criticism is not to be ignored; it must be reckoned with. The beginning point of reckoning with it is self-examination. Is the criticism directed to you as a person, or is it the position of leadership that is being questioned? Be honest. Does the criticism reflect some weakness or failure that you need to own and respond to, either in changes you need to make and/or response to the source of the criticism?

Sometimes we may need to defend ourselves, especially if truth is an issue. Truth telling and truth revealing are critical. If the criticism we receive has to do with style of leadership, we need to examine it carefully and determine if there are changes we need to make in order to be more effective.

Sometimes people are critical of us because of the "kind of person we are"—our personalities. Most of this does not call for defense. Sometimes, however, the person being critical needs to be confronted by our acknowledging to him or her: "Yes, this is who I am; I don't know if and how I need to change... but what ideas do you have, so that together we can get on with kingdom work?"

Our worst response, and least effective response to the "little fox" of criticism is to hunker down and assume the role of victim. Those who oppose and criticize us often have something to teach us. So, in response to criticism, we need to ask ourselves some questions: Is this something I need to hear, though I don't want to hear it? Is this criticism accurate, reflecting something for which I need to take responsibility? This kind of transparent honesty and deep listening will be refreshingly disarming to our critics and our most redemptive response.

Comparison and Competition

While the drive to achieve goals and further our careers may energize us to be our best, we often fall into the trap of "needing to win." Our winning need becomes the impetus for comparison and competition, which is one of the most cunning "little foxes" that spoils the vines. I name them together as one. If we named them singularly, they would have to be twins. It's difficult to talk about them separately. Comparison leads us to compete. Our competitive nature leads us to compare.

Jesus's original twelve disciples were a very competitive lot. Some dreamed of running the country. Brothers James and John openly maneuvered for a position on Jesus's anticipated cabinet: "Allow one of us to sit on your right and the other on your left when you enter your glory" (Mark 10:37 CEB). Jesus and the other disciples rebuked them for their competitive spirits. Jesus's rebuke in Mark 10:44 was anything but subtle: "Whoever wants to be first among you will be the slave of all."

Driven pastors are no different today—including me. By nature, I believe, we are competitive, and competition can be a hindrance to ministry. I have been involved in ministry for many decades, and my concern about competition is growing. It seems to me that social media feeds the temptation to compare. In a social media world, we can count the number of "likes" and "followers" and "tweets," so it is easy for ministry to become a popularity contest. No one likes to admit it, or talk about it, but it is so obvious we can't continue to ignore it.

I am not opposed to using social media in ministry; I tweet almost every day. It is a marvelous tool for ministry, but it can also be a dangerous tool for fostering a competitive celebrity spirit. It is a ready resource for our temptation to compare. Comparison fosters jealousy that other ministries are growing faster than mine, other churches are getting more press, other political groups are getting more followers, other pastors are more eloquent speakers and get more attention. This concealed jealousy fuels competition that is often not recognized and certainly not acknowledged.

Nothing is inherently wrong with ambition, but when it is coupled with competitiveness, it becomes a trap rather than an asset. If competitiveness is connected with the need to win, we judge our winning in how we compare with others. Perhaps unrecognized, that means we want to be number one. And that means others have to be numbers two or three or even exit the field. In 2 Corinthians, Paul dealt with the problems and limitations of comparison, insisting:

> We won't dare to place ourselves in the same league or to compare ourselves with some of those who are promoting themselves. When they measure themselves by themselves, and compare themselves with themselves, they have no understanding.
>
> We won't take pride in anything more than what is appropriate. Let's look at the boundaries of our work area that

God has assigned to us. It's an area that includes you. (2 Cor 10:12-13 CEB)

God sets the boundaries for our work area, and has given us unique gifts, skills, and talents. We need to bring those to the table as a valuable dimension of the partnerships God calls us into for accomplishing his kingdom work. To be sure, ambition may serve us well; it may lead us to hone those skills for cultivating relationships and collaborative functioning, all essential for leadership.

Whatever ministry or individual church we lead functions separately for practical reasons, but we must guard against the "little fox" who would have us compare and compete, and joyfully partner with others in accomplishing the mission of making disciples of Jesus Christ for the transformation of the world.

Each of us is a unique, unrepeatable miracle of God, vested with our own valuable gifts. We must be careful that, instead of praising God for who we are and our giftedness, we focus on the gifts of others, and ask him why we don't have those same gifts.

Playing a Role

Little foxes that destroy the vines are cunning. They come at us from different directions, enticing and tempting us in different ways. Though intimately connected with the dynamic of comparison and competition, playing a role needs particular consideration. Only a few pastors or ministry leaders find themselves free from the pitfall of playing a role. The pressure of this "little fox" is constant, because it consists of "playacting," which is a good translation of the Greek word *hypocrisy*.

Apart from our vocation, this is an issue in the whole of life. Even those who know us best, our loved ones and friends, have different role expectations for us. They have a certain image of us. In subtle and devious ways, they seek to manipulate us into being what they want us to be. We are tempted to be all things to all people.

Ross Snyder, in his book *On Becoming Human*, talked about "being a truth." "No one can be a center of self-propelling aliveness," he says, "who is not a truth" (Nashville: Abingdon, 1967). To be alive is to opt for being a truth rather than playing a role. For pastors and ministry leaders, it is very tempting to settle into the roles others design for us, to be swallowed up by their expectations.

Even Jesus experienced the pressure. The Pharisees wanted him to be a pious legalist. The Zealots cast him in the role of a militant revolutionary. His disciples wanted to mold and control him. Even after his bold affirmation, "You are the Christ, the Son of the living God," Peter couldn't let Jesus be himself. Following this confirmation, Jesus began to show his disciples "that he must go to Jerusalem and suffer...and be killed." It was Peter who objected, "God forbid, Lord! This shall never happen to you." With the sternness we often miss in him, Jesus vigorously rebuked Peter, "Get behind me, Satan! You are a hindrance to me" (Matt 16:16, 21-23 RSV).

We pastors and ministry leaders don't escape. We are victimized in at least two ways. One, we may try to respond to all the expectations and become quick-change artists—hypocrites—like chameleons that take on the color of our immediate environment. The chameleon can have a nervous breakdown if placed on a plaid coat that can't allow it to adjust to all the colors.

A second way we may be victimized is by looking at the innumerable expectations and selecting what we believe is the most viable one. Upon moving from one ministry setting to the next, we may take off our urban, slim-fit jeans and our casual shirt with the shirttail out, and don the buttoned-down-collar image to fit our new suburban, secular, sophisticated setting. Or, we may deliberately choose to not appear too "pious" and become more "worldly" by deliberately changing the language we use.

In many other ways, we get glued up in duplicity, which results in guilt, driven by the fear of being found out. Our energy is used in efforts to convince others that the "front" we are projecting is what we really are; but, like a shaven French poodle, we are never quite sure people are seeing us for who we actually are.

Like Jesus, we must not submit to the pressure of external expectation. In one of his most piercing words, he challenges us, "Why would people gain the whole world but lose their lives? What will people give in exchange for their lives?" (Matt 16:26 CEB). There is within each of us a self to be known and affirmed, to be cherished and developed to fulfillment. This is what Jesus was talking about. This is what it means to be a truth, and this is what integrity and character are all about.

CHAPTER 10

Time: It Is Ours to Receive, Use, and Manage

Sometimes time flies, sometimes it crawls, but it passes. We talk about saving it, wasting it, racing against it. We describe how we spend, save, or simply fritter it away. We say we believe it is precious. When Augustine was asked to describe it, he said: "If no one asks me, I know what it is. If I wish to explain it to him who asks, I do not know." There is a sense in which we are obsessed with time, yet we don't give it the kind of attention it deserves. The truth is, managing our time is really managing our life.

Calendars Are Essential

Calendars may be God's idea. We aren't two chapters into the Bible and we already have a calendar set around God's vision of time. God creates in six days and rests on the seventh. The first thing God declares holy is time itself. Yet we misuse time. We also waste it, either our time or others' time.

One of the greatest wastes of time is being late. We cheat ourselves out of some blessings. We also inconvenience others who are on time. We rob them as well as ourselves of precious moments as they sit waiting. I hardly ever go for an appointment, especially to a doctor, without a book or something to read. Even at this stage in life, I'm seeking to "redeem time." Paul instructs us to do that; "making the most of the time" is the way he put it (Eph 5:16 RSV).

How we need to heed this instruction. Few of us have proper balance in the use of time. Some of us are too frantically involved. We are like Lewis Carroll's white rabbit in *Alice in Wonderland*. With watch in hand, he kept muttering to himself in the presence of Alice, "I'm late! I'm late! For a very important date! No time to say hello, goodbye! I'm late! I'm late! I'm late!" We move from one thing to another, scheduling ourselves to the minute, without giving any thought to the quality of involvement, or the value of time. We allow what we consider urgent to rob us from doing the important, or enjoying the meaningful.

Just as sinful and destructive is the other extreme, the persons who make no commitments, who have no meaningful involvements, so they waste the precious time God gives all of us. For pastors and ministry leaders, how we manage time is an ever-present issue. Time management is one of the "little foxes that spoil the vines," but how we Christian leaders use our time calls for a more expansive consideration.

Peter Drucker, the late management guru, said, "Nothing else, perhaps, distinguishes effective executives as much as their tender loving care of time" (Drucker, *The Effective Executive* [1966], 76). The question is what we do with time, how we use it. Paul gives us some instruction as he uses athletic imagery to talk about his ministry:

> Don't you know that all the runners in the stadium run, but only one gets the prize? So run to win. Everyone who competes practices self-discipline in everything. The runners do this to get a crown of leaves that shrivel up and die, but we do it to receive a crown that never dies. So now this is how I run—not without a clear goal in sight. I fight like a boxer in the ring, not like someone who is shadowboxing. (1 Cor 9:24-26 CEB)

Busyness is not the issue; it's the purpose of our busyness, how we use our time that matters immensely. African leaders observe that each morning at dawn in the Serengeti, the gazelle must wake up running because it must run faster than the fastest lion in order to survive. On the same morning in the same Serengeti, the lion must wake up at dawn running in order to catch the slowest gazelle in order to survive. Both are running, both are very busy, but they know why they run.

The key phrase in Paul's imagery is "aimlessly" (9:26 RSV). Paul wants to stop us in our calendar tracks, forcing us to define "a clear goal" by reevaluating our schedules and determine what activities are worthwhile and what are simply aimless. To determine which is which requires intentional consideration.

In his distinctive style, the late motivational speaker Zig Ziglar challenged us: "If you will do what you ought to do when you ought to do it, then you can do what you want to do when you want to do it." Paul uses athletic imagery to talk about being busy with a purpose. In a race the runners all compete, but only one receives the prize. There is a purpose to Paul's busyness. He is not saying that running is the problem nor is it being too busy. Running aimlessly is the problem. We often need the involvement of some accountability partners to assist us in self-management.

I say, hopefully with generosity, that running full steam is not the problem with most pastors or active Christian leaders; too many of us are not running with purpose. We are not, as Paul instructed, "making the most of our time."

Some of us, early in our ministries, develop time-use patterns that do not serve us well as we are given larger and more demanding responsibilities. The common pattern is that we begin as pastors of small congregations. We can be effective leaders in those settings and have what we consider "spare" time. We can care for the pastoral concerns of our members, prepare "decent" sermons, and are not overwhelmed with weddings and funerals.

Instead of taking this season to develop a pastoral pattern and discipline of prayer and devotion, study, and sermon preparation that would serve us well throughout our life, we just "get by." We build a lifestyle of casualness in relation to time that cripples us for the rest of life if we don't overcome it.

Perhaps our most common failure is to schedule personal growth and spiritual formation time. Also, from years of observation I would say most pastors do not have a disciplined study and sermon preparation time. In terms of the ongoing life of a congregation and a congregation's growth as Christ followers, nothing is more important than worship, at the heart of which is preaching. We must schedule and protect time for our preparation.

In our calendaring, not only do we register church activities and events, we must schedule family and "play" time. Family vacations are important, and should be scheduled and valued, but they don't have the consistent quality of disciplined patterns of family togetherness. Nor is it enough simply to have a day off each week; special attention must be given to family. When children are school age, the minister father or mother being off from work one day a week doesn't make much time for children, as they are in school most of the day.

When Jerry and I get together with our adult children and grandchildren, conversation often turns to our early family life. What is remembered, and the stories told most, flow out of a ten-year period in our life together. It began when our son was preschool, and our two daughters were in elementary school. The only time I could be with them for more than an hour or two at a time was on Saturday. So we began a pattern of camping, sometimes two or three times a month, Friday night until four or five p.m. on Saturday (return determined by drive-time back home, and an occasional Saturday night wedding). We began with a tent, but it soon developed into a "pop-up tent trailer." We couldn't afford a different kind of camper, and there was nothing "fancy" about the tent trailer, but when you hear our family talking about those years and experiences, it may sound like we thought that time was sacred, and the tent trailer more than special.

Jerry and I would be ready to leave when the children got out of school on Friday; being in California, we could be at our favorite beach site within an hour, or in the mountains within two hours.

This required disciplined sermon preparation on my part; there was no waiting to put "finishing touches" on a sermon manuscript on Saturday. It had to be completed by Thursday. That discipline, forced by paying attention to family, has served my preaching life well.

How we spend holidays is important. For the sake of our children and family, holidays should not "just happen." Enriching, saving rituals can be connected with holidays. There was a ten-year season in our life when we were as "strangers in a foreign land." We moved from my home state, Mississippi, and Jerry's home state, Georgia, to California. Providentially, my father in the ministry, David McKeithen, and my closest college/seminary friend, Buford Dickinson, and their families were also in California during the same period. Our three families spent every Thanksgiving together. Those occasions were sacramental and life-giving for "sojourners in a foreign land."

The Overwork Trap

Though leaders early in ministry often develop patterns of sloppy time management, ironically it is also true that too many of us fall into the overwork trap. We are in trouble in our holiness and holistic pursuit if we spend every waking moment thinking about work. We don't have time for friends or exercise.

We don't give attention to healthy food and adequate sleep. We don't pay attention to our children. We go to work when we should stay at home because we are sick. We don't put ourselves in the shoes of those around us before we jump to conclusions in our assessment of them.

I'm quizzical when in a group where pastors and ministry leaders are claiming to sustain seventy- to eighty-hour workweeks. Overwork is seductive because it is too often lauded. Boston University's Erin Reid found that some people, men in particular, lie about how many hours they work, presumably thinking excessive hours impress those around them, especially their superiors. Many overworked leaders mistakenly believe that working more will alleviate stress. If they just finish that project, get that report done, read the latest must-read book, they'll feel less stressed and out of control. But the work never ends.

Annie McKee, author of *How to Be Happy at Work*, says,

> The good news is that some of the same leadership skills and mindsets that make you effective at work can help you escape and rediscover happiness there. The first step is to accept that you deserve happiness at work. That means giving up the misbelief that work is not meant to be a primary source of fulfillment.
>
> For centuries work was simply a means of staving off hunger. To be sure, many people still struggle with low wages and horrible working conditions, and for them, work may equal drudgery. But even menial jobs can provide fulfillment. (*Harvard Business Review* [September–October 2017]: 71)

I recently interviewed Baxter Richard Leach for our TV program, *We Believe in Memphis*. He is one of the few living men who was a part of the sanitation workers strike that brought Martin Luther King Jr. to Memphis. He was a part of the "I AM A MAN" demonstration. He didn't talk about the nature of his menial garbage collecting work, but he described why the workers were courageously demonstrating, and the commitment and meaning he had in supporting his family. Interestingly, when I asked him what word he would have for present-day young people, he underscored what he had talked most about: "Be a faithful worker, find meaning and stand up for what is right."

Deviation and Diversion

In battling the "little foxes that spoil the vines," we need deviation and diversion in our use of time. We are forced to deal with countless happenings, incidents, events, even persons who divert us from our normal schedules and well-ordered life. Despite those, maybe because of them, I believe we need to intentionally choose ways for deliberate diversion and deviation from our ordered life as leaders.

Cultivating a hobby is a common way of diversion. A hobby provides activity, interest, and enthusiasm, which gives us pleasure. It diverts us from stifling routine and can be a source of stress relief as well.

Early in my ministry, a seasoned pastor invited me for a round of golf. When I told him I didn't play golf, he responded, "Then you'll never be a success in the ministry."

Time: It Is Ours to Receive, Use, and Manage

I want to believe he was joking, but when I see the number of pastors whose favorite pastime is golf, I tend to believe he was serious. What I do know is that "healthy" leaders need planned, playful diversion from the daily grind of our stressful vocation.

The things you collect, in a sense, demonstrate what kind of person you are. Consistently throughout my life my primary diversion has been collecting artistic objects. On my limited income, one can't buy a painting too often, so consistently I have collected pottery, mostly Van Briggle. It is beautiful but not expensive. I could not number the times I have spent an hour in an antique store at 4 or 5 o'clock in the afternoon, following two or three stressful appointments, looking for a piece of Van Briggle.

In the past twenty years, I have often said facetiously, "We are art poor." But the truth is, we have been art "rich." We have enjoyed the "search" and the "find" of a piece both Jerry and I were attracted to, and we have enjoyed and been enriched with its presence (a painting, an icon, a bronze, a piece of pottery, a carving) in our home. As a part of our financial planning, we knew we would sell some of the pieces someday, and those days have come. We have sold some and have had the joy of giving many to our children and grandchildren.

In the ordering of our lives, we need to intentionally choose ways for deliberate deviation. The practice of these diversions will demand some calendaring, but some can be spontaneous if we are as sensitive to time as we should be.

Though calendaring and scheduling is important, it can be misused. We move from one thing to another, scheduling ourselves to the minute, without giving any thought to the quality of involvement, or the value of time. We must be careful and not allow what we consider urgent to rob us from doing the important, or enjoying the meaningful.

CHAPTER 11

Staying Alive All Our Ministry Life: Will You Finish Well?

Some experiences or encounters are so solidly lodged in our memory they continue to invade our consciousness. These memories may haunt us, help us, or hinder our Christian walk as they call and challenge us to be more than we are.

John Birkbeck is a person around whom for me such memories are gathered. John was a Scots Presbyterian preacher. During a part of my tenure as the World Editor of *The Upper Room*, he was the editor of the British edition of *The Upper Room*. He was a marvelous preacher in the classic style of the Scottish Divines.

I remember long walks in the evenings through the streets of Edinburgh, Glasgow, and Aberdeen. I remember extended hours across a table in a café over coffee—talking and talking and listening and listening. We were never together without my probing him about Christian doctrine, his own insight into biblical truth and preaching, and the wisdom of the Scottish Divines.

It was John who introduced me to the Scottish preacher Robert Murray McCheyne. He brought to my attention a word in one of McCheyne's books that has challenged me through the years: "The greatest need of my congregation is my own personal holiness."

I remember a time in my life in the early 1960s when I was confronted with this shocking fact: *I am as holy as I want to be.* It began in the midst of the civil rights upheaval in the South—and Mississippi was a powder keg. I was a young Methodist preacher in Mississippi. I was the organizing pastor of a congregation, which had known impressive growth. The congregation was a kind of Cinderella story, an inspiring demonstration of church growth. It became one of the success stories of Mississippi Methodism. During those days, there was no church growth literature, no testing of persons to see if they would make good leadership candidates for church planting. We did it intuitively, by the seat of our pants. I worked myself to the bone. I was worn out physically and emotionally. I kept asking myself a lot of questions: What is the difference between this congregation and the Rotary Club? Is there a quality of life here that is not present wherever people meet together? Why is it that most of these people have the same ideas about race relations that people outside the church have?

On and on the questions went. It was a tough time, and the fellowship of the church was splintered by my involvement in the civil rights movement. I didn't think there was anything radical about my involvement, but many folks in the church could not understand my commitment and participation. I couldn't understand their lack of understanding. The gospel seemed rather clear. The pressure, stress, and tension wore me out. I was physically, emotionally, and spiritually exhausted, and ready to throw in the towel. I even had thoughts about giving up the ministry.

My human resources were no longer adequate. Then it happened, a spiritual experience, clearly a Holy Spirit intervention, that sent me in a different direction than we had been going.

I went to a week-long retreat/conference, a Christian ashram, led by the missionary/evangelist E. Stanley Jones, mentioned in previous chapters. I will never forget going to the altar one evening, to have Brother Stanley lay hands on and pray for me. We had shared together during the week, so he knew my story. As I knelt, he asked me a probing question in two ways: "Do you want to be *whole*? Do you want to be *holy*?"

That was a signal sanctifying experience in my life, changing forever the direction of my ministry. Through the years since I have constantly asked myself, "Do I want to be holy?" And I have constantly reminded myself that I am as holy as I want to be.

On-Course Adjustments Essential

Our calling and our performance in ministry require mid-course adjustments all along the way. Growth and learning are essential for life, critical for the survival of the individual and the community. Psychologist Eric Erickson says that in midlife we face a choice between stagnation and generativity. Stagnation happens when we are threatened and we barricade ourselves behind our status, our title, our notion that we are good enough where we are and have no reason to push any further. Generativity, conversely, is about creativity and the endless emergence of the new.

The choice between stagnation and generativity may begin, as Erickson says, in midlife. However, especially now that over one-third of congregations are led by second-career or bi-vocational leaders, I have seen the tension between stagnation and generativity emerge earlier.

It was 1968 in Mexico City. John Stephen Akhwari of Tanzania had started the Olympic marathon with all the other runners hours before, but he finished it alone. When he finally arrived at the stadium there were only a few spectators remaining in the stands. The winner of the marathon had crossed the finish line over an hour earlier.

It was getting dark; his right leg was bandaged and heavily bleeding. He was obviously in great pain, but he crossed the finish line suffering from fatigue, leg cramps, dehydration, and disorientation. A reporter asked him why he didn't just quit. He thought for a moment and said, "My country did not send me here to start the race; my country sent me here to finish it."

For all, especially for Christian leaders, finishing well is important. I'm eighty-three years old as I write this. I make no claims about success, but I can say without hesitation, I am finishing well. In fact, knowing that you are finishing well means that you have not yet finished.

The description of life as a race in the Letter to the Hebrews is an appropriate and challenging metaphor for leadership as vocation.

> So then let's also run the race that is laid out in front of us, since we have such a great cloud of witnesses surrounding us. Let's throw off any extra baggage, get rid of the sin that trips us up, and fix our eyes on Jesus, faith's pioneer and perfecter. He endured the cross, ignoring the shame, for the sake of the joy that was laid out in front of him, and sat down at the right side of God's throne. Think about the one who endured such opposition from sinners so that you won't be discouraged and you won't give up. (Heb 12:1-3 CEB)

The beginning of the text is an uplifting reminder at every stage of our ministry: we are surrounded by a great cloud of witnesses.

In Hebrews 11, the writer gives us a list and description of Old Testament heroes of the faith. The letter is remembering this multitude ("cloud"), some of whom suffered and sometimes died for their faith.

That certainly harmonizes with Jesus's and Paul's talk about heaven and the resurrection of the body. That's the reason I like to talk about the resurrection of the body rather than immortal life. Immortality is really a Greek idea, though we took it over into the Christian faith. The unique Christian idea is the resurrection of the body. When I get to heaven, I want to know and greet my friends and my family; I want to hug them, and I want them to hug me. I want to greet them and experience in an ongoing way what I experience fleetingly now and then in what we call the communion of the saints.

When we're surrounded by a great cloud of witnesses, the communion of saints, we do not live our lives in isolation, and we do not walk our journey to spiritual wholeness alone. Not only are we surrounded by our earthly friends and supporters but witnesses who have gone on from this earthly scene are with us.

Sometimes when I'm in my study preparing to preach, sometimes even when I get into the pulpit, I get a sense of the presence of my grandfather, Lewis Dunnam, who was an uneducated Freewill Baptist preacher, who preached the gospel under severe physical handicaps and personal difficulties; and according to all who knew him, preached it with power, making all the sacrifices necessary to do so. And sometimes when I grow weary, trying to respond to all the human needs that are constantly coming to the church, and to me as pastor—when I grow weary in that and think I can't continue, I get a vision of my brother, Lloyd. He was two years older than me. In 1975, at age forty-three, he went down into the hold of a ship to save some men who were overcome with poison gas and he died, seeking to save them. You see, we're surrounded by persons who have made their witness, who have lived their discipleship, and who now share in the glory of the Lord.

It's not enough for me to experience that fleetingly, and to think of it only in terms of those who have gone before. The writer of Hebrews moves from past faithfulness to present striving in a seamless transition. Athletes were also "surrounded" by witnesses when the great coliseums of the day filled up for some sports spectacular.

As witnesses to the gospel, we are standing with people right now who are seeking to make the same witness, some of them suffering the threat of death as they do. The terminology reflected in the great Greek games was intense: wrestling, agonizing, contending. In fact the word for "race" is the Greek word *agon*, from which we get the English word *agony*. Keeping this awareness of a "cloud of witnesses" enables us to stay alive all our ministry life and finish well.

Hebrews also provides an explicit call to living daily in a way that guarantees that we finish well: run with perseverance the race marked out for us. Other nouns meaning "perseverance" are *endurance, resolution, determination*, and *stubbornness*. In more colloquial idioms, *die-hard* and *bulldogged* would express the meaning.

I'm at the age when I can look back and plot the zigzag course of my journey and hopefully share a bit of wisdom for those who are beginning, as well as for those who have been at it for a while and have made the saving discovery that our calling and our performance in ministry require on-course adjustments all along the way, with perseverance being the key.

Mastery of Our Moods

A look at one area of ministry life will make the case. The very nature of our work makes us vulnerable to drastic moods, and one of our disciplined responses to life must be the mastery of our moods. Consider one of the most common moods: discouragement. It manifests itself in the greatest of leaders. You remember Moses. At one time he would express his willingness to die for his people. "Oh, what a terrible sin these people have committed! They made for themselves gods of gold. But now, please forgive their sin! And if not, then wipe me out of your scroll that you've written" (Exod 32:31-32 CEB).

That's the same person—willing to die for his people—who at another time wanted to die in order to get away from them. Listen to him in the book of Numbers. Again he's speaking to the Lord:

> Moses said to the LORD, "Why have you treated your servant so badly? And why haven't I found favor in your eyes, for you have placed the burden of all these people on me? Did I conceive all these people? Did I give birth to them, that you would say to me, 'Carry them at the breast, as a nurse carries an unweaned child,' to the fertile land that you promised their ancestors? Where am I to get meat for all these people? They are crying before me and saying, 'Give us meat, so we can eat.' I can't bear this people on my own. They're too heavy for me. If you're going to treat me like this, please kill me. If I've found favor in your eyes, then don't let me endure this wretched situation." (Num 11:11-15 CEB)

It's times like these, times that involve our seeking to lift others, and keep their eyes focused on "higher things," that we have our turn trying to conquer the destructive moods of discouragement in our own life.

Moffatt's wonderful translation of Job 4:3-5 describes our situation: "You have yourself set many right, and put strength into feeble souls; your words have kept men on their feet, the weak-kneed you have nerved. But now that your turn has come, you droop; it touches you close and you collapse?" We know about that, don't we? I offer two suggestions that may help us triumph over the deadly mood of discouragement.

First, we need to recognize that the mood of discouragement is often the psychological reaction to extreme mental and physical fatigue. When you're seeking to deal with discouragement, be sure that you are adequately rested.

Second, discouragement often results from an impractical idealism, an illogical attempt at perfectionistic activity. I know about that. You will be hard-pressed to find a more optimistic, idealistic person than me. Yet, how often have I had to cry out, "Oh, hopeless idealist that I am: who will deliver me from the bondage of believing that in this life all ideals can become realities?"

We need to constantly make a valid distinction between philosophical idealism and moral responsibility. Just because we know all that can be done, and just because we desperately want to do it, does not necessarily mean that we have to do it. Sometimes doing what we see needs to be done may transcend our human capacity, particularly when other human beings are involved. Our human judgment will not suffice. We must cultivate attention to the Holy Spirit's guidance to lift us out of discouragement, but also to guide us in making on-course adjustments in our pattern of life and ministry.

I witness to this in my own life. I quoted Thomas Fuller in chapter 8. I owe him an enthusiastic expression of gratitude.

Chapter 11

He provided a warning that was so important to me that I put a date on it in May 1992. I came upon his word in my devotional reading, memorized it, and it has become a kind of motto for me. *Let not thy will roar when thy power can but whisper.*

Throughout my life, until a few years ago, I had a recurring dream. The dream expressed itself in different ways, but always there was the same dynamic. It all centered in my deep feelings of inferiority, my inadequacy, and my drive to be an effective preacher. In my dream I would need to be somewhere to preach. Sometimes I would be at home; the service of worship was to begin in ten minutes and I would be struggling to button the collar of my shirt, unable to do so, knowing that I was running out of time.

Or I wouldn't be able to tie my tie. Or I might discover that the cleaner had mixed up my clothing and I would put on a pair of pants and find the coat didn't match. Or even discover that the pants might be two or three inches too short. Or that I couldn't button them around my waist—all sorts of silly, irrational things that would be preventing me from getting to the church in time to preach.

The dream expressed itself in all sorts of ways that demonstrated my struggle, my fighting, the pressure and the stress, the driven intensity of my life—all circling around my own feelings of inadequacy and unpreparedness, as well as the limitations of my past, yet with the drive for perfection.

I had not had a dream like that for many years. But it happened again and it was so dramatic and disruptive I recorded the date in my journal, Tuesday night, July 27, 1993. I felt as though the dream went on all night long. When I woke at five o'clock in the morning, I was in a sweat, completely worn out. There was no logic to the dream, but it was the same dynamic: my feelings of inadequacy and unpreparedness, as well as the limitations of my past, yet with the drive for perfection.

After my morning time of prayer, I went to my office that day totally exhausted, but having received a message from God, a message to surrender, to let go. In retrospect, I knew why I had had the dream. I was the chair of the committee on evangelism for the World Methodist Council, and I was supposed to leave that coming Sunday to visit congregations in the Czech Republic, to speak at a conference in Estonia, and to visit a congregation in Russia. I was also chairing the board of trustees and the search committee to find a new president for Asbury Theological Seminary. That process was just getting underway and was a huge responsibility. I was working on a book manuscript, which had a deadline six weeks later.

A lot of things were going on in the life of our congregation, Christ United Methodist in Memphis. We were growing and expanding in so many ways, adding new staff and planning a building expansion. The opportunities for ministry were almost overwhelming. On top of all that, my mother had had a stroke the Sunday afternoon preceding the dream.

So God was speaking to me again, and on that Wednesday morning I renewed my commitment to the Lord. The word from Thomas Fuller, which I had underscored in a book I had been using in my devotional time some months before, and which had been God's word for me, came alive. At the risk of irreverence, I say, "The word became flesh. Let not your will roar when thy power can but whisper."

I renewed my commitment to God. I canceled my travels to Eastern Europe and Russia. I said to the Lord that I was going to do my best and be a responsible chairperson for the search committee at Asbury, but I was not going to get all stressed out about it. I accepted the fact that it would not be catastrophic if I missed my book deadline, and I committed my mother to the Lord. I would continue to be the best leader I could for my congregation in Memphis, but I was not going to carry all the weight of it on my shoulders. God doesn't intend that for any one of us.

So I surrendered. I realized again how limited I am and how dependent I am upon the Lord; how yielded I must be to God if his power is going to be perfected in my weakness. The line that I had marked in my devotional reading had been made powerfully alive by my dream: "Let not your will roar when your power can but whisper." After I surrendered, about eight months after Fuller's word had gotten my attention, I accepted the presidency of Asbury Theological Seminary, a ministry I never anticipated and for which I felt totally inadequate.

I grew up in severe poverty in Perry County, Mississippi. I never knew how many years my mother and father went to school, but I knew they never attended high school. I felt myself culturally, socially, and intellectually deprived. In reaction to that, I developed an almost sick determination to achieve, to get out of that situation, to be a success. So I spent a great part of my life driving myself unmercifully. I accepted the call to lead the seminary, kicking and screaming inside, because I became convinced it was God's will for this particular season of my life.

We must cultivate attention to the Holy Spirit's guidance to lift us out of discouragement, but also to guide us in making on-course adjustments in our pattern of life and ministry. It takes perspective to make those course corrections.

Spiritual, emotional, and relational growth takes time and energy. It requires discipline. It diverts us from "pastoral duties," which will eat us alive if we don't keep perspective. When we begin our ministry life, we're enthusiastic for God and we want nothing more than to be sterling men and women of God. Whether it's due to our seminary training, or ecclesiastical machinery, or competition among pastors, early on we're tempted to become increasingly preoccupied with success. We start climbing the ladder, looking for a bigger church, a bigger salary, and greater recognition.

Later in ministry, we realize how we have strayed. It's not that we have ignored spiritual growth and character development completely, but we've not had the time or inclination to concern ourselves with it.

Somewhere along the way, most of us awaken to the fact that we have not kept perspective. If we have not forsaken our first love, we certainly have not kept that love alive. We've not given it first place. Unfortunately, many of us are in our forties and fifties before we come to this realization.

To keep personal and ministry growth perspective, we must remember that all the permanent fruit and progress

Chapter 11

that result from our leadership are based on strong character. We considered this earlier when we talked about calling and character. Who we are is more crucial than what we do.

Ministry Has Potential of Handicapping Character

Here may be a shocking fact for your reflection: our ministry has the potential to handicap our character. Although the average parishioner thinks being a pastor makes it easier to grow character, we know otherwise. Vocational ministry can dry and stiffen the red clay of the human spirit for several reasons.

The need for job security is one of these. We explored this with respect to ambition and competition in chapter 9. Now in the context of finishing well, how much of our ministry, the tone and direction of our ministry, is shaped by this need? Congregations can be fickle. Staff/parish relations committees can be unrealistic and demanding. Too many churches demand far more of their leader than is possible.

Without conscious awareness, this need for job security significantly affects how we do ministry, especially with the finish line in view. It certainly blunts the prophetic edge of our ministry. I began this chapter sharing about my ministry, during the racial upheavals in Mississippi in the late 1950s and early 1960s, during which I had taken a clear stand in the civil rights movement, which brought me into direct conflict with many folks in the church. At one point, the leaders held a special board meeting to confront the issue, some supporting and others opposing me.

After the meeting had gone on for some time, one opponent who wielded substantial power in the congregation, asked, "Well, Maxie, what can we expect of you in the future?"

The response had to be the Spirit working within me. I heard myself saying, "You can expect me to be consistent with what I feel the gospel is calling me to do."

I wish I could claim I have always been that clear in my convictions, and always that strong. It simply hasn't been the case. All of us, when we are honest, probably would confess that our need for job security has shaped our ministry. That becomes a handicap for character-building.

Akin to this is a second reality: the frequent moves of pastors from one congregation to another. When we are constantly moving from one congregation to another every two, three, or four years, we don't have the opportunity to clarify troubling issues, or work through recurring problems in our own personhood and character. And with so many working pastors and leaders (77 percent of clergy over age fifty-five) in or nearing retirement, concerns multiply for future security in that last appointment.

High and unrealistic expectations are another hindrance, even right up until we reach the finish line. I remember a story about a woman who approached the great Scottish preacher Alexander Whyte, complimented him profusely, and said, "Oh, Dr. Whyte, if I could just be as saintly as you are!"

"Madam," he replied, "if you could see into my heart, you would spit in my face."

We may fear that if people discover who we really are, we're finished, or at a minimum, our credibility and influence will wane. The human reflex is to hide, put on a mask. Hypocrisy is the greatest temptation of religious professionals. As we discussed in the last chapter, our temptation is to play a role rather than be the unique persons God wants to use in his kingdom enterprise.

The opposite of high expectations from oneself and from others is settling in to limited expectation as we finish the race. Some people don't want us to be too Christian, who by word and deed are calling people to more Christlike behavior. They want us to be merely nice, fulfilling our role with reasonable skill and efficiency. Under that expectation, it's easy to become complacent. Instead of striving to become all that Christ calls us to be, we simply do what is expected of us: regular hospital calls, decent sermons, warm blessings at women's groups. Ministry may certainly be that much—but it is far more.

While staying aware that our ministry has dimensions that thwart character development and growth in holiness, we can deal with the temptations that come with our vocation by continually asking ourselves questions like these:

- Am I resisting image-building by living as transparently as possible?
- Am I dealing with the self-deceit that comes from the applause of others?

- Am I keeping my calling clear, resisting both the temptation for security and a competitive spirit?
- Am I defensive when asked questions about the use of my time and the consistency of my spiritual disciplines?
- Am I blaming others for things that are my own fault and the result of my own choices?

I restate the claim from previous chapters. All the permanent fruit and progress that result from our leadership are based on strong character. Yet it's not enough to recognize that the fruit and progress that result from our leadership are based on strong character; we must practice the disciplines that build that character.

A Treasure in Earthen Vessels

In the introduction, I told the story of Groucho Marx's reaction to his opportunity to be a part of the elite Friars' Club. He stated, "I don't care to belong to any club that will have me as a member" (*The Groucho Letters* [New York: Simon and Schuster, 2007], 8).

That's the way I sometimes feel about ministry. How is it that I'm here? What did God have in mind? How could it be that the Lord would put a hand on my shoulder and beckon me in this specific call?

Paul voiced this same kind of concern:

> We don't preach about ourselves. Instead, we preach about Jesus Christ as Lord, and we describe ourselves as your slaves

for Jesus' sake. God said that light should shine out of the darkness. He is the same one who shone in our hearts to give us the light of the knowledge of God's glory in the face of Jesus Christ.

But we have this treasure in clay pots so that the awesome power belongs to God and doesn't come from us. We are experiencing all kinds of trouble, but we aren't crushed. We are confused, but we aren't depressed. We are harassed, but we aren't abandoned. We are knocked down, but we aren't knocked out.

We always carry Jesus' death around in our bodies so that Jesus' life can also be seen in our bodies. (2 Cor 4:5-10 CEB)

One of the ways I stayed alive in ministry, and maintained a sense of balance and perspective, has been by constantly appropriating this witness of Paul—the image of the treasure in a clay jar.

Paul's second letter to the Corinthians in which we find this image is one of the most personal letters we have in the New Testament. Paul is hurting in his relationship with the Corinthians, and he wants to change the conversation and the relationship. He wants the Corinthians to know of his love for them, and of the necessity of their believing and receiving the gracious love of Jesus Christ. He emphasizes to the Corinthians that the purpose of his visits with them is not about him. The purpose is rather about the God he knows in Jesus Christ: "We don't preach about ourselves. Instead, we preach about Jesus Christ as Lord." Throughout the entire letter, Paul emphasizes as strongly as possible that the theme of his engagement with the Corinthians is not Paul and his personality but the power of the gospel of Jesus Christ.

In chapter 7, we discussed the preacher and preaching, and made the case that the gospel is communicated through the person. Yet here, Paul's distinction between himself and the proclamation of the gospel helps to focus on an important issue: our own limits. We need one another for edification, for comfort, and for caring; but when we begin to see the gospel and/or our leadership as defined and confined to our point of view, we are proclaiming ourselves, not Christ.

These words from Paul are both astonishing words of grace and careful words of caution. God's work is not confined to us, or totally dependent on us; we must be cautious and careful that we do not try to contain or constrict God. Paul reinforces this with his expressive phrase: "We have this treasure in clay pots."

The metaphor of an ordinary clay jar carrying something of great value makes a clear distinction between the messenger and the message, between the pot and its content.

We are to remember our "ordinary" status; we are not the treasure. Yet, we are not to be defined by our ordinary status but by the precious cargo we have been asked to carry and to share: the grace of Jesus Christ.

By God's Mercy

Paul begins 2 Corinthians 4 with a powerful reminder: "This is why we don't get discouraged, given that we received this ministry in the same way that we received God's mercy" (CEB).

This brings us back to our previous discussion in chapters 1 and 2 about the nature of our *calling*. As we each contemplate our call and examine our ministry all the way to the finish line, our heart should beat faster. And it is almost impossible to enter into this kind of reflection about ministry without verse 5 of our Corinthian lesson coming to mind: "We don't preach about ourselves. Instead, we preach about Jesus Christ as Lord, and we describe ourselves as your slaves for Jesus' sake." When I have a resonance of being at my best as God's servant, everything inside trembles. As I become conscious of this awesome vocation that is mine, if I don't say it out loud, I feel what Paul was saying in verse 7: "But we have this treasure in clay pots so that the awesome power belongs to God and doesn't come from us."

The primary way we think and talk about this is *sense of calling*. I have no doubt about it; God's call has been confirmed over and over again in my life. And, had I not kept that call alive, I doubt I'd be in the ministry today.

I've been dubious over the years, while serving in groups responsible for affirming persons as candidates for ordained ministry, or when interviewing perspective leaders for staff positions, as I've heard young men and women give as their rationale for being a minister, "I want to help people." That's a prerequisite—but that's not a sufficient reason for being in the ministry. All Christians ought to be motivated to help people. But something more is needed if we're going to live out a representative ministry for the whole people of God and throughout the whole of life. We've got to stay sensitive to God's call.

We've all seen pastors who've lost "the appetite for ministry." Some are burned out, which can be healed through discipline with use of time. But some Christian leaders become cynical. They do their job. They are successful. They operate within the system in such a way as to guarantee advancement. But there's no "cutting edge" in their life—no contagious excitement, no passion about what they're doing, which will not let them sit down, or stay quiet, as it relates to their calling. The calling has died.

A phrase of Paul's, which is a favorite of mine, describes ministry as we who are ordained should perceive it: stewards of God' grace. "Each of you should use whatever gift you have received to serve others, as faithful stewards of God's grace in its various forms" (1 Pet 4:10 NIV). In the Bible a steward is a person who supervises a household or manages someone's affairs. For Paul, Christian leaders are "good managers of God's diverse gifts" (CEB).

A Heart for God

Recently a friend excited me by saying: "That person really has a heart for God." That's what I want people to be able to say about us who are stewards of a great treasure in these earthen jars of clay.

Frank Harrington, longtime minister of Peachtree Road Presbyterian Church in Atlanta, was a person whose life and ministry overflowed with stewardship. The last time I was with Frank, before his death, I told him a story about my mother-in-law and father-in-law, who lived in Atlanta. Frank was one

Chapter 11

of their favorite television preachers. One Sunday morning as they listened, they bolted upright in surprise by Frank referring to their son, Randy.

Randy had died of cancer a few years before. I had written about Randy's death in one of my books, and quoted a letter that Randy had written me in the midst of his suffering with cancer. Frank read that letter in my book and used it as an illustration in his sermon and he mentioned mine and Randy's names. You can imagine how that took my wife's parents by surprise.

The week Frank was back in Atlanta, after I told him the story, he called my in-laws and shared a pastoral visit over the phone. He had thousands of people in his congregation and a national television ministry, yet he took the time to call two people whom he'd never met and shared with them the love of Christ.

Early in his ministry, Frank started practicing the disciplines that developed his character. When he went to college, he was a candidate for the ministry under the care of Harmony Presbytery in South Carolina. Once a year he had to appear before the presbytery in person to give an account of his progress, his plans, and his studies. In retrospect, he said, "there's only one thing I remember about those appearances. Mr. Knox, an older white-haired minister, would get up and ask the same question every time I was there. 'Frank, are you making any progress in your walk with Christ?'" That's the sort of question we must never stop asking ourselves, and to answer it well.

The life of Mother Teresa is another example of sustaining a sense of calling, even during times when she became discouraged or was beset with doubt. A brother in a religious order came to Mother Teresa complaining about a superior whose rules, he felt, were interfering with his ministry. "My vocation is to work for lepers," he told her. In a voice of desperation, he said, "I want to spend myself for the lepers."

She looked penetratingly at him for a moment, then smiled gently, saying, "Your vocation is not to work for lepers, your vocation is to love Jesus."

Staying aware of that foundational claim, that our vocation is to work for Jesus, knowing that we are stewards of God's grace, keeps our appetite for ministry vividly alive, and we will finish well.

CPSIA information can be obtained
at www.ICGtesting.com
Printed in the USA
LVHW041952051218
599397LV00003B/3

9 781501 883118